understood it before. It was full of money—that was t
austible charm that rose and fell in it, the jingle of
nbals' song of it. . . . High in a white palace the kin
er, the golden girl. . ."Her voice is full of money," he sa
ly. That was it. I'd never understood it before. It was fu
y—that was the inexhaustible charm that rose and fell
jingle of it, the

F. Scott Fitzgerald

the king's daugh
ey," he said sudde
It was full of
se and fell in it, the jingle of it, the cymbals' song of
gh in a white palace the king's daughter, the golden gi
voice is full of money," he said suddenly. That was it.
understood it before. It was full of money—that was t
austible charm that rose and fell in it, the jingle of
nbals' song of it. . . . High in a white palace the kin
er, the golden girl. . ."Her voice is full of money," he sa
ly. That was it. I'd never understood it before. It was fu
y—that was the inexhaustible charm that rose and fell
jingle of it, the cymbals' song of it. . . . High in a wh
the king's daughter, the golden girl. . ."Her voice is fu
y," he said suddenly. That was it. I'd never understood
It was full of money—that was the inexhaustible cha
se and fell in it, the jingle of it, the cymbals' song of
gh in a white palace the king's daughter, the golden gi
voice is full of money," he said suddenly. That was it.
understood it before. It was full of money—that was t
austible charm that rose and fell in it, the jingle of
nbals' song of it. . . . High in a white palace the kin
er, the golden girl. . ."Her voice is full of money," he sa
ly. That was it. I'd never understood it before. It was fu
y—that was the inexhaustible charm that rose and fell
jingle of it, the cymbals' song of it. . . . High in a wh
the king's daughter, the golden girl. . ."Her voice is fu
y," he said suddenly. That was it. I'd never understood
It was full of money—that was the inexhaustible c
se and fell in it, the jingle of it, the cymbals' song

exhaustible charm that rose and fell in it, the jingle of
laughter, the golden girl. . ."Her voice is full of money," he

F. Scott Fitzgerald

Kevin Alexander Boon

Marshall Cavendish
Benchmark
New York

With thanks to Professor Jackson R. Bryer,
professor of English at the University of Maryland,
for his expert review of this manuscript.

Marshall Cavendish Benchmark
99 White Plains Road
Tarrytown, NY 10591
www.marshallcavendish.us

All Internet sites were available and accurate when sent to press.

Library of Congress Cataloging-in-Publication Data
Boon, Kevin A.
F. Scott Fitzgerald / by Kevin Alexander Boon.
p. cm. — (Writers and their works)
Summary: "A biography of writer F. Scott Fitzgerald, that describes his
era, his major works, his life, and the legacy of his writing"—Provided by publisher.
Includes bibliographical references and index.
ISBN 0-7614-1947-0
1. Fitzgerald, F. Scott (Francis Scott), 1896-1940. 2. Authors,
American—20th century—Biography. I. Title. II. Series.
PS3511.I9Z5584 2005
813'.52—dc22
200402344

Photo research by Linda Sykes Picture Research, Hilton Head, SC

Cover Photo: Granger Collection

The photographs in this book are used by permission and through the courtesy of:
Granger Collection: 2; Manuscripts Division, Department of Rare Books and Special Collections,
Princeton University Libraries: 12, 16, 17, 18, 19, 21, 24, 29, 33, 39, 41; Bettmann/Corbis: 47, 53;
Underwood and Underwood/Corbis: 10, 51; Leonard de Selva/ Corbis: 56; PARAMOUNT/
The Kobal Collection/The Picture Desk: 62, 92, 96.

Series design by Sonia Chaghatzbanian

Printed in China

135642

Contents

YB Fitzgerald, F. Bo

r voice is full of money," he said suddenly. That was it.
er understood it before. It was full of money—that was t
exhaustible charm that rose and fell in it, the jingle of
e cymbals' song of it. . . . High in a white palace the kin
ughter, the golden girl. . ."Her voice is full of money,"
d suddenly. That was it. I'd never understood it before.
s full of money—that was the inexhaustible charm that r
d fell in it, the jingle of it, the cymbals' song of it. .
gh in a white palace the king's daughter, the golden girl
er voice is full of money," he said suddenly. That was it.
er understood it before. It was full of money—that was
exhaustible charm that rose and fell in it, the jingle of
e cymbals' song of it. . . . High in a white palace the kin
ughter, the golden girl. . ."Her voice is full of money,"
d suddenly. That was it. I'd never understood it before.
s full of money—that was the inexhaustible charm that r
d fell in it, the jingle of it, the cymbals' song of it. .
h in a white palace the king's daughter, the golden gir
er voice is full of money," he said suddenly. That was it.
er understood it before. It was full of money—that was
exhaustible charm that rose and fell in it, the jingle of
e cymbals' song of it. . . . High in a white palace the kir
ughter, the golden girl. . ."Her voice is full of money,"
d suddenly. That was it. I'd never understood it before.
s full of money—that was the inexhaustible charm that r
d fell in it, the jingle of it, the cymbals' song of it. .
h in a white palace the king's daughter, the golden gir
er voice is full of money," he said suddenly. That was it.
er understood it before. It was full of money—that was
exhaustible charm that rose and fell in it, the jingle of
e cymbals' song of it. . . . High in a white palace the ki
ughter, the golden girl. . ."Her voice is full of money,"
d suddenly. That was it. I'd never understood it before.
s full of money—that was the inexhaustible charm that r
d fell in it, the jingle of it, the cymbals' song of it.
h in a white palace the king's daughter, the golden gir
er voice is full of money," he said suddenly. That was it.

Introduction

"Something in his nature never got over things, never accepted his sudden rise to fame, because all the steps weren't there."

(F. Scott Fitzgerald, *The Romantic Egoists*, 80)

F. SCOTT FITZGERALD IS ONE OF THE KEY AUTHORS of the modern period of American literature (1914–1945). His name stands alongside those of Ernest Hemingway, William Faulkner, and others as one of the most significant writers and literary personalities of the period.

Fitzgerald achieved success and fame early, becoming a well-known author in his early twenties, but his life was troubled and his death at age forty-four was tragic. He may have been a victim of early wealth and fame as implied in the above quote from his notebooks, or he may have been too self-absorbed to last beyond the indulgent decades of his youth, as noted by Heywood Broun in a 1920 interview with Fitzgerald. Summarizing his impression of the young writer, Broun writes, "Having heard Mr. Fitzgerald, we are not entirely minded to abandon our notion that he is a rather complacent, somewhat pretentious and altogether self-conscious young man" (1920, 5).

Fitzgerald's contributions to American literature and American culture are unarguable. His lifestyle in the 1920s and his novels and short stories shaped and reflected the age. His novel, *The Great Gatsby*, which some consider the great American novel, has become a national literary treasure.

It is fair to say that F. Scott Fitzgerald in his life and his work often placed his faith in the most superficial values: youth, wealth, and popular success. Yet, his talent was such that his brilliant command of language and his insight into human character rendered works of enduring quality.

Part I:
The Life of
F. Scott Fitzgerald

FLAGPOLE SITTING BEGAN IN 1924 WHEN HOLLYWOOD STUNTMAN, ALVIN "SHIPWRECK" KELLY, ON A DARE, SAT ON A POLE FOR THIRTEEN HOURS AND THIRTEEN MINUTES. HIS FEAT DREW WIDESPREAD ATTENTION AND LAUNCHED A NATIONAL CRAZE TO SEE WHO COULD SIT ATOP A POLE THE LONGEST. KELLY EVENTUALLY CLINCHED THE TITLE AFTER SITTING ON A POLE FOR FORTY-NINE DAYS.

Chapter 1

A Well-Worn Life

THE STORY OF F. SCOTT FITZGERALD is more than the story of a single man. It is the story of a particular slice of American history that falls between The Great War (World War I, 1914–1918) and the Great Depression (1929–1939). This historic decade, alternately referred to as "The Jazz Age" and "The Roaring Twenties," has often been characterized as a period of economic prosperity, elevated spirits, and shifting cultural mores. Charlie Chaplin, Rudolph Valentino, and Clara Bow ruled the box office. Al Capone fueled Chicago speakeasies with bootleg liquor, because the Prohibition Act made the sale of alcohol illegal in the United States. Charles Lindbergh made a historic nonstop solo flight across the Atlantic Ocean in the *Spirit of St. Louis.* Harry Houdini wowed fans by escaping from straitjackets and prison cells. Women won the right to vote. Babe Ruth swatted home runs for the Yankees. It was the heyday of dance marathons, jazz music, flagpole sitting, Mah-Jongg, rolled silk stockings, and young women with bobbed haircuts. It was a period in American history that Fitzgerald both helped shape and chronicled in his writing.

Childhood

Fitzgerald was born Francis Scott Key Fitzgerald on September 24, 1896, in St. Paul, Minnesota. Scott's mother, Mollie Fitzgerald (née McQuillan), descended from Irish-Catholic immigrants. Her father prospered as a wholesale dealer in the grocery trade. His fortune would

F. SCOTT FITZGERALD, AGE TWO, RIDING A HOBBYHORSE.

keep Scott's parents financially afloat after Scott's father, Edward Fitzgerald, failed at several attempts to establish himself in business. Edward's great-great-grandfather was the brother of Francis Scott Key, Scott's namesake, an American lawyer and part-time poet who composed a poem during the War of 1812 that became the lyric for "The Star Spangled Banner."

The first years of Scott's life were colored by grief and loss. The occupants of the three-story brick house at 481 Laurel Avenue were in mourning the afternoon that Scott was born. Mollie and Edward Fitzgerald had two daughters, both of whom died from illness about three months before Mollie gave birth to Scott. Fitzgerald associated the tragedy with his career as a writer. Although his mother never spoke of the deaths of her first two children, Scott claimed he felt the effects. A little more than three years later, another sister was born into the family. She lived only one hour. Just before Scott turned five, his sister Annabel was born and he was no longer the only child in a house full of ghosts.

Several early factors foreshadowed Scott's later adult life.

• Scott developed a sense of style that he got from his mother, who was particular about the way she dressed him, and his father, who was a meticulous dresser.

• Scott had an impressive memory and ability to recall much of what he experienced. This would contribute to his sparkling talent for sensory detail in his writing.

• Scott had a knack for language and he loved to read, which helped him develop a large vocabulary at a young age.

• Scott had the ability to quickly understand and explain why people behaved the way they did. This talent, although important in his writing, ironically would not help him avert disaster in his personal life.

• Scott's mother frequently moved the family to new houses, establishing a pattern of transience that Scott would duplicate throughout his life as he moved across America and Europe, from hotels to rented houses to villas and estates, seldom satisfied for very long with one home.

• Scott developed an early identification with Princeton University. After hearing the Princeton Glee Club sing a hilarious version of "Mrs. Winslow's Soothing Syrup," Scott became enchanted by the school. By the age of nine, he was announcing that he would be attending Princeton when it was time for him to go to college.

Scott adored his father despite his father's inability to succeed in the business world. Scott recounts the day his father lost his job with Procter & Gamble as one of the most traumatic in his life. Scott was eleven. When he learned that his father may have lost his job, he prayed, "Dear God . . . please don't let us go to the poorhouse." He writes of his father that day:

> That morning he [Scott's father] had gone out a comparatively young man, a man full of strength, full of confidence. He came home that evening an old man, a completely broken man. He had lost his essential drive, his immaculateness of purpose. He was a failure the rest of his days. (Turnbull, 1962, 17)

The family moved back to St. Paul, Minnesota, to be near Mollie's family and the McQuillan fortune. Money from the McQuillans kept the family in large homes with servants. In 1913, when Scott was sixteen, Grandmother McQuillan died and Scott's mother inherited $125,000, which was enough to keep his parents in good circumstances for the rest of their lives. Despite Edward Fitzgerald's failures and Mollie Fitzgerald's contributions to the economic welfare of the family, Scott preferred his father and was embarrassed by his mother's lack of social graces.

St. Paul Academy and The Newman School

F. Scott Fitzgerald began writing while a student attending St. Paul Academy in St. Paul, Minnesota. A fan of live theater, sports, and literature, Scott began acting in plays and writing for the school newspaper. His first publication was "The Mystery of the Raymond Mortgage" in the October 1909 edition of *Now and Then*, a St. Paul Academy student publication. Scott was thirteen. He published three more stories the next year: "Reade, Substitute Right Half," "A Debt of Honor," and "The Room with the Green Blinds."

Although Scott excelled at writing and acting, he performed poorly in other subjects. He also loved sports, although he never achieved more than an occasional moment of athletic brilliance on the field. His admiration for the sports heroes at all the schools he attended influenced the characters he created in his stories and later novels, many of whom were physically powerful and accomplished athletes.

Scott was only fourteen when his first work was performed on stage. A theater group made up of Scotts' friends and supervised by one of his teachers (The Elizabethan Dramatic Club) staged Scott's first play, *The Girl from Lazy J*, in St. Paul. Fitzgerald starred in the production and served as stage manager. The Elizabethan

CAST PHOTOGRAPH FOR *THE COWARD*, WHICH FITZGERALD
WROTE AND HELPED DIRECT IN 1913.

Dramatic Club would go on to produce three more of young
Scott's plays: *The Captured Shadow, The Coward* (which
Scott helped direct), and *Assorted Spirits*. All four plays displayed their author's talent for clever, witty dialogue.

Scott entered the Newman School in Hackensack,
New Jersey, at the age of fifteen. He was not popular. His
personal philosophy, which he later referred to as "a sort
of aristocratic egotism," made his first year socially difficult. Nevertheless, Scott maintained his enthusiasm for
life. He was determined to succeed. He even managed to
secure a place as second-string quarterback on the football team. But Scott was bossy and condescending, which
left him on the outs with most of the student body.
However, he continued to write. He published poetry and
stories in the school newspaper, the *Newman News*. Soon
he discovered that he could overcome his social and athletic shortcomings by proving himself in print.

HIGH SCHOOL PHOTOGRAPH OF F. SCOTT FITZGERALD.

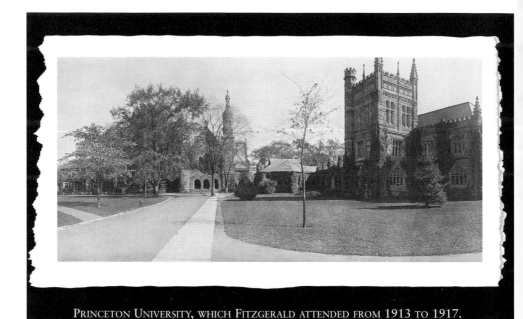

PRINCETON UNIVERSITY, WHICH FITZGERALD ATTENDED FROM 1913 TO 1917.

Princeton

Scott was greatly concerned when his grades were too low for admittance to Princeton. Even after he retook a number of exams, he still did not have enough credits for admission to the university. However, his scores were close enough to allow him to appear before the admissions committee and plead his case. He was approved for admission on the condition that he make up credits.

Elated by the news, Scott immediately wired his mother to send his football pads, assuming that he would join the football team where he would win glory for himself and his new alma mater. He lasted three days on the team. At 5'7" and 135 pounds, he was simply too small for collegiate football.

Scott's focus returned to his writing, which had served him so well at Newman and St. Paul Academy. The primary outlets for his talent were a humor publication called *The Tiger* and a theater group known as the Triangle Club, which created and produced musical comedies. As before, his coursework took second place to his literary interests. Although Fitzgerald would write lyrics for three of the Triangle Club's productions, he was barred from performing in them because of his low grades. Nevertheless, several reviews of the 1914 production of *Fie! Fie! Fi-Fi!*, including those in the *Louisville Post* and the *Baltimore Sun*, praised Fitzgerald's clever and witty lyrics.

ADVERTISEMENT FOR A TRIANGLE CLUB PRODUCTION AT PRINCETON, FEATURING F. SCOTT FITZGERALD DRESSED AS A CHORUS GIRL.

In 1915, Scott began to publish works in *Nassau Literary Magazine*. He had one play and one short story in print there by November of his junior year, when he fell so far behind in his studies that he dropped out of Princeton. He returned the next year.

Fitzgerald's first significant relationship with a woman had occurred while he was at Princeton. From 1915 to 1917, he was involved with Ginevra King, a wealthy socialite from Lake Forest, Illinois. According to Don C. Skemer, the curator of manuscripts for the Princeton library's Rare Books and Collections department, Ginevra King was "for Fitzgerald an archetype for the alluring, independent and upper-class woman, ultimately unattainable by someone of a modest social background" (Stevens, 2003) like Fitzgerald. Many scholars believe that King was Fitzgerald's model for Daisy in *The Great Gatsby*. Like King and Fitzgerald, Daisy and Jay Gatsby were from different worlds, just as King in her letters makes it clear that her social status would prevent marriage to Fitzgerald (although she confessed that she loved him), Daisy's social status prevents her from marrying Jay Gatsby.

World War I was raging and Scott wanted to get in on the action. In November of 1917 he was commissioned as a second lieutenant in the infantry and the following month was sent to Fort Leavenworth in Kansas for officer training.

Military Days

At Fort Leavenworth, Fitzgerald approached military study with the same lack of interest with which he had approached his classes at Princeton. He slept through lectures and generally made a bad impression. He was not a good officer (though he was convinced he was destined for glory on the field of battle).

GINEVRA KING WAS F. SCOTT FITZGERALD'S FIRST LOVE. SHE IS BELIEVED TO HAVE BEEN THE MODEL FOR DAISY BUCHANAN IN *THE GREAT GATSBY.*

Fitzgerald continued writing while at Fort Leavenworth. Convinced that he would die in battle, he began work on the novel that would eventually become *This Side of Paradise*. The book was originally titled *The Romantic Egotist*. He completed a draft in three months and in March 1918 sent it to Irish writer Shane Leslie, who forwarded it to Scribners. That same month Fitzgerald was placed in charge of a company of the Forty-fifth Infantry Regiment stationed at Camp Taylor in Kentucky. In April the regiment was moved to Camp Gordon in Georgia. In June the regiment was again moved to Camp Sheridan in Alabama. Fitzgerald was promoted to first lieutenant.

In July Fitzgerald met the woman who was to become an inseparable part of his life and subsequent legend— Zelda Sayre, the grandniece of one senator, granddaughter of another, and daughter of an Alabama Supreme Court judge. Scott was twenty-one. Zelda was just turning eighteen. They met at a country club dance where Fitzgerald was charmed by her uninhibited, impetuous nature. He began making regular visits to her home in Montgomery.

Scribners sent back *The Romantic Egotist* in August with numerous suggestions for revision. Fitzgerald hastily rewrote the manuscript and sent it back to Scribners in October, the same month he was transferred to Camp Mills in Long Island for embarkation.

Scribners rejected Fitzgerald's manuscript a second time, asking him to not submit it again. Fitzgerald's only consolation was the enthusiastic comments of one of Scribners' editors— Maxwell Perkins, with whom Fitzgerald was to develop a lifelong relationship.

Fitzgerald had mixed feelings about going overseas. He was looking forward to combat, but afraid he would never see Zelda again. Long Island was the last stop before being shipped out. When his division was ordered overseas, Fitzgerald made it onto a ship for Europe, but before the ship could leave shore, the war ended and

Fitzgerald came back on land. With a mixture of regret and relief, he had missed the war. He was discharged on February 18, 1919. He immediately headed for New York City to become a successful writer.

Early Romance and Zelda

Zelda's contributions to F. Scott Fitzgerald's life and work cannot be overestimated. Not only was she the love of his life and his companion throughout his most successful and notorious years, she was also the source of much of his inspiration. Shortly after they met, Zelda shared her diary with Fitzgerald, portions of which showed up in two of his novels (*This Side of Paradise* and *The Beautiful and Damned*) and at least one of his short stories ("The Jelly Bean").

Fitzgerald and Zelda had a great deal in common. They were both attractive and looked enough alike that some people said they could pass for brother and sister. More important, they were both exuberant about life and vibrantly interested in adventures among the well-heeled. They also possessed similar weaknesses. Jackson R. Bryer and Cathy W. Barks note in the preface to their edited collection of Fitzgerald and Zelda's love letters, "Although Zelda and Scott married young, their inherited predispositions to mental illness and alcoholism, respectively, were already present. These traits were apparent in the impulsive behavior that characterized their courtship and actually fed their attraction for each other from the beginning" (Bryer and Barks 2002, xv).

> Both of us are very splashy, vivid pictures, those kind with the details left out, but I know our colors will blend, and I think we'll look very well hanging beside each other in the gallery of life. —Zelda Sayre
>
> (From a letter to F. Scott Fitzgerald, Milford, 1970, 59)

ZELDA SAYRE (1919), FROM FITZGERALD'S *THIS SIDE OF PARADISE* SCRAPBOOK.

Just as Fitzgerald felt he was socially beneath Ginevra, Zelda may have felt she was from a lower social order than Fitzgerald. Her biographer, Nancy Milford, claims Zelda saw Fitzgerald as "a new breed of man. . . . He represented a world she did not know and could not hope to enter, much less possess, without him" (Milford 1970, 36). Other scholars contend that Zelda felt no difference in social standing.

Despite what may or may not have been a perceived difference in social standing, it is clear from the numerous letters they exchanged throughout 1918 and 1919 that the two were in love. They got engaged in February of 1919.

Life in New York was unpleasant for Fitzgerald. He could not find work as a newspaper journalist as he had first planned and wound up writing copy for an advertising agency. The stories he was writing were not selling and his self-confidence suffered. He pleaded with Zelda to marry him right away, saying that he needed her, but Zelda was shaken by his failure and refused him, breaking off their engagement and sending him back to New York alone.

Fitzgerald responded to this rejection by immediately quitting his job and going on a drinking binge that lasted three weeks. He joked that his alcoholic tailspin was only stopped by the arrival of Prohibition (July 1, 1919). Determined to get his novel published, he headed back to his parents' house in St. Paul to rewrite his manuscript.

By the end of September, Scribners agreed to publish Fitzgerald's revised novel, now called *This Side of Paradise*, and Fitzgerald had his first literary sale—he sold "Babes in the Woods" to *The Smart Set*. In October, he sold his first of many short stories, "Head and Shoulders," to *The Saturday Evening Post*. He also wrote Zelda telling her of his success and asking for permission to come visit. Zelda agreed and the two once again got engaged.

They were married in the rectory of St. Patrick's Cathedral in New York City on April 3, 1920, just after the publication of Fitzgerald's first novel, *This Side of Paradise*. Zelda was nineteen and Scott was twenty-three.

"Writing Prose, Anything Goes!"

Zelda and Fitzgerald honeymooned at the Biltmore Hotel in New York City. Money was coming in now that Fitzgerald's writing had begun to sell. Fitzgerald had gotten into the habit of spending it carelessly even before Zelda joined him. The $2,500 he had received for the movie rights to his short story, "Head and Shoulders," had all gone to buy Zelda a platinum and diamond wristwatch. Friends recall twenty- and fifty-dollar bills carelessly strewn about Fitzgerald's hotel room.

The Fitzgeralds embraced their new life with abandon. Fitzgerald performed handstands in the lobby of the fashionable Biltmore Hotel. Fitzgerald and Zelda raced hand-in-hand down Fifty-seventh Street. New York for the Fitzgeralds was, as Andrew Turnbull describes it, "the playground of a younger generation that was tired of Great Causes, at odds with its elders, full of energy stored up by the war, and determined to be amused" (Turnbull 1962, 109). Their antics during their honeymoon got them thrown out of the Biltmore, so they moved to the Commodore and continued in the same manner as before.

Prohibition was in effect, but speakeasies were plentiful and the Fitzgeralds spent a great deal of their time drinking. It was a habit they had indulged since their first days in Montgomery, and one Fitzgerald would continue for the rest of his life. Everything they did, they did to extremes. When they loved, they loved deeply. When they fought, they fought with vigor. When they drank, they drank to excess—and they drank a lot. Drinking was inextricably part of their flamboyant lifestyle.

They moved to Westport, Connecticut, for the summer so that Fitzgerald could write and Zelda could swim, but they continued their party life. Zelda rarely cleaned the house or did laundry, and Fitzgerald refused to do these tasks, so they frequently lived in a pigsty. The alcohol continued to flow freely.

By the time they moved back to New York in October, Fitzgerald had begun work on a new novel, *The Beautiful and Damned*. The Fitzgeralds rented an apartment near the Plaza Hotel where they could take easy advantage of room service. Fitzgerald now earned $20,000 a year (equivalent to around $184,000 by contemporary standards). Yet, because of his unchecked spending, he was still desperate for cash. Often, when he needed funds to stay ahead of creditors, Fitzgerald would borrow money from his editor at Scribners, Maxwell Perkins, in advance against stories he was going to write.

> "[H]ow wonderful it is to be young and beautiful and a success!"
>
> —F. Scott Fitzgerald
> (Turnbull 1962, 126)

A collection of his short stories called *Flappers and Philosophers* was published in September of 1920, resulting in Fitzgerald mistakenly receiving credit for coining the term "flapper." Fitzgerald used the term to describe the new woman of the 1920s. She was young, adventurous, and liberated from the chaste mandates of the previous century. Fitzgerald also claimed credit for naming the Jazz Age. In a letter to Maxwell Perkins, Fitzgerald writes, "I claim credit for naming it [The Jazz Age] . . . it extended from the suppression of the riots on May Day 1919 to the crash of the stock market in 1929—almost exactly one decade." The Jazz Age was the period of Fitzgerald's greatest fame, his peak marketability, and his and Zelda's closest times together.

In 1921 Zelda and Fitzgerald visited Europe. They had planned on settling down in Montgomery when they returned, but they found Alabama weather unsuitable. They decided instead to set up housekeeping in St. Paul, Minnesota, where their only child, a daughter, Frances Scott "Scottie" Fitzgerald, was born on October 26. Zelda was as uninterested in buying baby clothes and furniture as she was in housekeeping. Her stance was that "children shouldn't bother their parents, nor parents their children" (Bruccoli & Baughman 2004, 48). When asked what she wanted for her daughter, Zelda Fitzgerald replied, "Not great and serious and melancholy and inhospitable, but rich and happy and artistic. I don't mean that money means happiness, necessarily. But having things, just things, objects makes a woman happy. The right kind of perfume, the smart pair of shoes. They are great comforts to the feminine soul" (Bruccoli & Baughman 2004, 49).

In 1922 Fitzgerald's second novel, *The Beautiful and Damned*, was published after first being serialized in *Metropolitan Magazine*. Toward the end of the year, a second collection of short stories (*Tales of the Jazz Age*) was published and the Fitzgeralds moved to Great Neck, Long Island, where they set up house, complete with a nurse, a laundress, a pair of housekeepers, and a Rolls Royce. They threw legendary parties there.

In 1923, in addition to his usual outpouring of stories, Fitzgerald wrote an unsuccessful play (*The Vegetable*). That year their income reached a new high of nearly $29,000 (equivalent today to about $313,000), but they spent $36,000 (equivalent to about $389,000, or, "20 times the average income in the United States" (2001, 129). Fitzgerald was forced to continue borrowing

THE FITZGERALDS (SCOTT, ZELDA, AND SCOTTIE) CELEBRATING CHRISTMAS IN PARIS IN 1925.

money. Fitzgerald disliked writing what he considered trashy stories for magazines such as *The Saturday Evening Post*, but his continual overspending forced him to continue writing whatever would earn him the most income. Nevertheless, he dreamed and talked of writing the great American novel. In a letter to Perkins at Scribners (whom he frequently hit up for advances), Fitzgerald wrote:

> [M]any thanks for all deposits, to you and to the Scribners in general. I have no idea how I stand with you. To set me straight, will you send me my account now instead of waiting till February 1st? It must be huge, and I'm miserable about it. The more I get for my trash, the less I can bring myself to write. However this year is going to be different. (Turnbull, 1963, 195)

Drink, Disagreement, and Decline

By 1923 alcohol had already become a serious problem for Fitzgerald. He tried to quit, but couldn't do it. He would sometimes go on binges and disappear for several days, often returning with no memory of where he had been or what he had done. Zelda also drank to excess, but it was Fitzgerald's behavior that was most negatively affected by drink. Music and drama critic Carl Van Vechten spoke of Fitzgerald's weakness for the bottle:

> He could take two or three drinks at the most and be completely drunk. It was incredible. He was nasty when he was drunk, but sober he was a charming man, very good looking, you know, beautiful, almost. But they both drank a lot—we all did, but they were excessive. (Milford, 98)

Zelda and Scott's relationship was strained by alcohol and excessive partying. The Fitzgeralds drank when they fought and fought when they drank.

In 1924 they headed back to Europe where they met Gerald and Sara Murphy. The Murphys represented the ideal to which the Fitzgeralds (especially Scott) aspired. They had inherited a great deal of money and were extremely wealthy. They were also young, vibrant, and attractive. The Murphys helped acquaint Zelda and Fitzgerald with the French Riviera, which the Fitzgeralds both adored. Scott settled into a daily writing schedule while Zelda spent her days on the beach. Eventually, Zelda began sharing her days with Edouard Jozan, a handsome French aviator, and a relationship blossomed. The Murphys suspected the affair before Scott, but in July Zelda told Scott she was in love with Jozan and asked him for a divorce. Fitzgerald refused, insisting on a direct confrontation with Jozan. The confrontation never took place and Zelda reconciled herself to her life with Fitzgerald. Years later, Jozan denied ever having an affair with Zelda. He claimed that the Fitzgeralds "both had a need of drama, they made it up and perhaps they were the victims of their own unsettled and a little unhealthy imagination" (Milford, 112). Whether an affair actually took place or was merely imagined by Zelda, it is clear that Fitzgerald believed that it had.

Despite the growing tension between Scott and Zelda, Fitzgerald completed a draft of *The Great Gatsby* by the end of the year. In 1925 *The Great Gatsby* was published to mixed reviews. Some critics recognized it as a significant literary work; others panned it. Edwin Clark wrote in his *New York Times* review, "The philosopher of the flapper has escaped the mordant, but he has turned grave. A curious book, a mystical, glamourous story of today. It takes a deeper cut at life than hitherto has been essayed by Mr. Fitzgerald" (Clark 1925, BR9).

Fitzgerald was disappointed in its sales. Shortly after the book's release, the Fitzgeralds rented an apartment in Paris and Fitzgerald met the American author Ernest Hemingway for the first time.

Fitzgerald was awed by Hemingway. Fitzgerald, who since his success had been supportive of other young writers, helped Hemingway establish a professional relationship with Scribners. Fitzgerald admired Hemingway for many reasons, among them Hemingway's dedication to his art, his strong physical presence, and his writing. Hemingway had many of the characteristics that Fitzgerald lacked but had long wished he had. Hemingway was athletic; he had served in the war; and he was a disciplined writer. Fitzgerald was never particularly good at athletics (though he greatly admired men who were), and he failed to see action during the war. Furthermore, he wasted large amounts of time on frivolity and drink when he should have been writing. Even when he was writing, he often worked on popular pieces that would earn him quick money rather than pursuing more serious fiction. According to one of Fitzgerald's biographers, "Hemingway was a literary version of the bloodied and bandaged football heroes Scott had worshiped in college" (Meyers 1994, 134).

Hemingway introduced Fitzgerald to other "expatriates" and key figures in The Lost Generation, including Gertrude Stein, who was charmed by Fitzgerald. In *The Autobiography of Alice B. Toklas*, Stein writes, "Gertrude Stein had been very much impressed by *This Side of Paradise*. . . . She said of it that it was this book that really created for the public the new generation. She has never changed her opinion about this. She thinks this equally true of *The Great Gatsby*. She thinks Fitzgerald will be read when many of his well known contemporaries are forgotten" (Kazin 1951, 9).

ERNEST HEMINGWAY (FAR RIGHT) IN FRONT OF SHAKESPEARE AND COMPANY, A WELL-KNOWN LITERARY HANGOUT IN PARIS DURING THE 1920S. THE BOOKSTORE WAS OPERATED BY SYLVIA BEACH (ON HEMINGWAY'S LEFT).

The Hemingways and the Fitzgeralds were friends of a sort, though the friendship was based primarily on the relationship between the two writers—Ernest and Fitzgerald—and their shared interest in literature. Zelda did not take to Ernest, as Fitzgerald had hoped she would, and reportedly called him "bogus" when she met him. Ernest thought Zelda was crazy.

Zelda's behavior had become erratic at times. The Murphys spoke of her peculiar habit of occasionally breaking out into fits of strange laughter. One incident occurred when the Fitzgeralds were dining with the Murphys in the mountains above the French Riviera. Fitzgerald showed too much attention to Isadora Duncan, who was seated at a nearby table. In a moment of jealousy, Zelda "stood up on her chair and leaped across both Gerald and the table into the darkness of the stairwell behind him" (Milford 1970, 117). Zelda re-emerged bloodied but calm after tumbling down the flight of stone steps.

The money continued to roll in despite Zelda's declining mental state and Fitzgerald's unrestrained drinking problem. In 1926, *The Great Gatsby* was adapted for the stage and had a successful run at the Ambassador Theatre on Broadway, and another collection of short stories, *All the Sad Young Men*, was published. At the end of the year, the Fitzgeralds headed back to the United States.

Hollywood, Ballet, and Booze

In January of 1927, Fitzgerald and Zelda traveled to Hollywood where Fitzgerald worked on *Lipstick*, an unproduced flapper movie that was to star actress Constance Talmadge. Fitzgerald disliked Hollywood, but he was charmed by a seventeen-year-old actress named Lois Moran. The relationship between the two never extended beyond harmless flirtation, but Zelda resented Fitzgerald's attraction to Lois. At the heart of the problem was the fact that Fitzgerald had for years complained about Zelda's inactivity and her lack of independent accomplishment. In Lois he saw someone full of promise, a young woman who was succeeding on her own merits. One night while Fitzgerald and Lois dined together, Zelda took all of her dresses, many of which she had designed herself, placed them in the bathtub of their bungalow at the Ambassador Hotel, and set them aflame. After United Artists rejected Fitzgerald's screenplay, the two took the train back East. On the way, they got into another fight about Lois Moran, and Zelda heaved the platinum and diamond wristwatch Fitzgerald had given her before their wedding out of the window of the moving train.

Back on the East Coast, the Fitzgeralds rented "Ellerslie," a twenty-seven room mansion in Wilmington,

Delaware. The plan was to avoid the distractions of New York City and settle down for a time in a peaceful setting where Fitzgerald could focus on writing his novel. The plan was ill-fated. The Fitzgeralds continued to throw wild parties, inviting guests out for the entire weekend. Zelda's behavior became more erratic; she grew distant and removed. She was painting and writing (with Fitzgerald adding his name before hers on some of the works she published) and frantically practicing ballet. Fitzgerald's excessive drinking became even more extreme. Until their move to Ellerslie, Fitzgerald had only drunk when he was not writing. Now he began drinking in order to be able to write.

The marriage bent under the stress. Zelda and Fitzgerald often bickered with one another. Zelda sometimes practiced ballet eight to ten hours a day, seven days a week. Fitzgerald would go on binges. Zelda would complain to Fitzgerald about his drinking, and Fitzgerald would harass Zelda about her dancing. By March of 1928, they were sick of life at Ellerslie. They traveled back to Paris for the summer. On the way, Zelda accused Fitzgerald of having a homosexual relationship with Ernest Hemingway.

In Paris, Fitzgerald's drinking worsened and Zelda at twenty-seven began ballet lessons with Madame Lubov Egorova. Fitzgerald wrote very little by the end of summer and described the period as one of "drinking and general unpleasantness" and "general aimlessness and boredom" (Milford 1970, 142). On at least one occasion, he struck Zelda during a row.

In September they returned to Ellerslie. Zelda immediately resumed her ballet routine. Fitzgerald took to drinking and boxing with a French taxi driver and ex-boxer he had brought back with them from Paris to serve as their chauffeur. Zelda continued to write, Fitzgerald continued to drink, and the two had numerous angry scenes witnessed by family and friends. They headed back to Europe in March of 1929.

> Zelda's father "said to her, 'I think you better divorce him—you can't make a life with a fella like that' . . . Zelda said he was the sweetest person in the world when sober, to which her father replied, 'He's never sober.'"
>
> —Zelda Fitzgerald and her father
> (Turnbull 1970, 204)

In June, Fitzgerald sat in as timekeeper for a boxing bout between Ernest Hemingway and Canadian novelist Morley Callaghan. Fitzgerald accidentally let a round go an extra minute, during which time Callaghan knocked Hemingway down. Hemingway blamed Fitzgerald, accusing him of intentionally not calling the match on time. Hemingway, who had a reputation for long-lived grudges, never forgot the incident. It formed a wedge between the two writers that would last for the rest of their lives.

By the end of 1929, Fitzgerald had become a social embarrassment with his drinking and antics, and everyone had begun to notice Zelda's strange behavior. Zelda was continuing her ballet and continuing to write and publish, with Fitzgerald still adding his name to many of her stories, presumably to increase the amount of money they earned. Fitzgerald was writing and publishing too, but mostly short stories to earn quick money and stay ahead of his debts.

They visited North Africa in February of 1930. They returned to Paris a couple of months later, and Zelda had a mental breakdown. While lunching with friends who were visiting from St. Paul, Zelda suddenly became frantic about missing a ballet lesson. She got up in a state of extreme agitation and hailed a taxi. One of her friends went with her to ensure that she was all right. On the way, Zelda changed in the taxi and when the taxi stopped momentarily at a crossing, Zelda jumped from the auto and ran to the studio. The friend told Fitzgerald about Zelda's bizarre behavior and Fitzgerald had her admitted to a Paris hospital on April 23. Slightly more than a week later, Zelda checked herself out against her doctor's advice. She immediately returned to ballet. She began to hear voices and experience hallucinations. Within two weeks, she could only be calmed with a shot of morphine.

Zelda was placed in Valmont Hospital in Switzerland, where the doctors' report noted,

> the husband's [Fitzgerald's] visits often were the occasion of violent arguments, provoked especially by the husband's attempts to reason with the patient and to refute the patient's insinuations suspecting the husband of homosexuality. . . . It was evident that the relationship between the patient and her husband had been weakened for a long time and that for that reason the patient had not only attempted to establish her own life by the ballet . . . but that she also [had withdrawn] from her husband. (Milford 1970, 159–160). Zelda was transferred to Prangins Clinic in Nyon, Switzerland, for psychiatric treatment.

In January of 1931 Fitzgerald's father died. Fitzgerald traveled to America to attend the funeral. Zelda began to improve in Fitzgerald's absence. When he returned, he continued to pump out short stories to cover the cost of Zelda's expensive psychiatric care. It took him four to six days for each story, during which time he would lock himself in his room and avoid alcohol. By September, Zelda was well enough to leave the sanitarium, and the Fitzgeralds headed back to America. They visited New York City for a few days and found it much changed. The carnival of the 1920s was over. The stock market crash and changing attitudes had calmed the city so much that it no longer seemed to Fitzgerald to be the vibrant center of his universe.

The Fitzgeralds moved to Montgomery, Alabama, and rented a house. Fitzgerald hoped for a calmer, more productive life there. At the end of the year, Fitzgerald headed back to Hollywood for eight weeks to work on a screenplay for *Red-Headed Woman* for MGM (Fitzgerald's screenplay was rejected). Despite the hardships of 1931, it would be the year Fitzgerald achieved a career high in earnings, taking in $37,599 (equivalent to about $455,000 today).

Zelda and Scott in Decline

In February of 1932, when she was thirty-one, Zelda had another breakdown. Suffering from hallucinations, she was admitted to Phipps Psychiatric Clinic of Johns Hopkins University Hospital in Baltimore, Maryland, where she completed her novel, *Save Me the Waltz,* and pursued her painting with renewed vigor.

In March she sent her novel directly to Perkins. Fitzgerald was upset and contacted him, complaining that large portions of the manuscript were influenced by the work Fitzgerald was doing on his novel. He forced a revision to eliminate all the sections he felt impinged on his artistic territory. The manuscript was revised to Fitzgerald's satisfaction, and he was ultimately proud of her accomplishment.

Scribners eventually agreed to publish Zelda's novel with the stipulation that half of her royalties go to repay

Fitzgerald's existing debt to the publisher. *Save Me the Waltz* was published in October and earned a total of $120. Meanwhile, her artwork had begun to attract interest. She had an exhibition in Baltimore, one of several she would have over the next few years, including one in New York City.

Fitzgerald moved to "La Paix," a house in Towson, Maryland, just outside of Baltimore, to be near Zelda. He found it increasingly dif-

"Self Portrait" by Zelda Fitzgerald (pastel drawing)

ficult to earn the level of income to which he had become accustomed. His income in 1932 dropped 50 percent from the previous year. In 1933 Zelda's play, *Scandalabra*, was produced in Baltimore by the Vagabond Junior Players. It was poorly received. The Fitzgeralds moved yet again, this time from La Paix to a smaller house in Baltimore.

By 1934 Zelda had a third breakdown and was committed to Sheppard-Pratt Hospital in Towson and then transferred to Craig House Hospital in Beacon, New York. Fitzgerald's novel, *Tender Is the Night*, was finally finished. It was serialized in *Scribners Magazine*. In April, the novel was published to good reviews and strong sales, but Fitzgerald, expecting more, was once again disappointed. Zelda, who had been transferred back to Sheppard-Pratt Hospital, was "a little upset" (Milford 1970, 286) after she discovered that Fitzgerald's *Tender Is the Night* contained excerpts from her private letters and dealt explicitly with her mental illness. She later praised the book.

In 1935 another short story collection was published (*Taps at Reveille*), but Fitzgerald was in decline. His excessive drinking and chain-smoking had begun to take their toll, and writing had become a constant struggle for him. Fitzgerald's confidence had failed and Zelda suffered long periods during which she was incoherent and wholly withdrawn. By the end of the year, Zelda developed religious delusions and claimed that the end of the world was approaching and she was working with God to teach mankind. In 1936 Zelda was transferred to the Highland Hospital in Asheville, North Carolina. Fitzgerald moved to Asheville to be near her.

Fitzgerald frantically tried to keep writing, although he was fearful that his talent was gone. Ernest Hemingway published a story that ridiculed Fitzgerald ("The Snows of Kilimanjaro") and claimed that his career was over. Fitzgerald, who had never stopped admiring Hemingway, was devastated.

An alcoholic in failing health and desperate for money, Fitzgerald jumped at an opportunity to return to Hollywood under a six-month contract to MGM at $1,000 a week.

Fitzgerald's Last Days in Hollywood

In July of 1937 Fitzgerald—at the age of forty—returned to Hollywood. Fitzgerald had been married to Zelda for seventeen years, when, a week after arriving in Hollywood, he met Sheilah Graham, with whom he would be involved for the remaining years of his life. Fitzgerald was a shadow of his former self. The man who had been a vibrant, dynamic icon of the roaring twenties had become a timid, nervous man. Fitzgerald worked diligently on the screenplays he was assigned, though he often bickered with cowriters and producers about the artistic merit of his scriptwriting and hated knowing that his work was frequently rewritten by lesser writers. Nevertheless, in December MGM renewed his contract for another year at $1,250 a week.

> "A writer not writing is practically a maniac within himself."
>
> —F. Scott Fitzgerald
> (Turnbull, 298)

FITZGERALD AND SHEILAH GRAHAM IN MEXICO.

Fitzgerald worked on many screenplays during the year and a half that he was under contract to MGM, but only received one screen credit—for the film *Three Comrades*. At the end of the year, MGM did not renew his contract and he was forced to freelance. In February of 1939 he was hired to work on *Winter Carnival*, but during a trip to Dartmouth College to research the Dartmouth Winter Carnival for the film, Fitzgerald got drunk and made a spectacle of himself. He was fired from the project.

In July Fitzgerald terminated his relationship with his agent, Harold Ober, when Ober refused to lend him more money. Fitzgerald sold stories where he could and in the summer he began work on a new novel (*The Last Tycoon*) partially based on the life of Irving Thalberg (a young and successful movie producer during the early days of film). Fitzgerald tried desperately to generate more income while working on the book, but to no avail. His ability to sell his work with ease had eroded and he was, in his last days, tired, broken, and depressed.

Fitzgerald also had physical ailments to contend with, some real and some imagined. Arthur Mizener points out that Fitzgerald "had always been hypochondriacal when he was drinking . . . any steady drinking made him very ill, and any drinking at all became steady drinking" (1974, 309).

On December 21, while eating a chocolate bar and making notes in the *Princeton Alumni Weekly*, he jerked to his feet, grabbed the mantelpiece, and then, gasping for breath, dropped to the floor—dead at the age of forty-four. The new book remained unfinished.

A Decade of Decadence: The Roaring Twenties

F. SCOTT FITZGERALD'S PRINCIPAL WORKS in the 1920s chronicled the spirit of the age. His works in the 1930s noted its passing. Fitzgerald's writing is linked to that unique period in American history referred to as the Roaring '20s and the Jazz Age. Arthur Mizener notes that "Fitzgerald had an imaginative sense of the experience of the 1920s, was indeed a writer so closely related to his time that he was in danger of being wholly absorbed by his sense of it and of writing books that would not survive it" (Mizener 1973, 99–100).

Fitzgerald's popularity and early success as a writer resulted from his ability to capture the mood of the times through sensory descriptions and captivating narratives. More than any other writer, Fitzgerald was the biographer of the 1920s, and one of its most central figures. An understanding of America during the 1920s helps us to better appreciate Fitzgerald's contribution to American literature.

Mass Production

The first part of the twentieth century witnessed an increase in the mass production of goods. The principles of mass production lessened the need for skilled labor. The most visible figure in this movement was Henry Ford, who began in 1905 to plan factories for the production of automobiles. The benefits of this assembly-line method of mass production were that the bulk of the work could be completed by unskilled labor and products could be built quickly and much more efficiently.

The impact of this new method of production on the 1920s was twofold. It created a large number of affordable modern conveniences, such as automobiles, refrigerators, radios, and so on, and it gave weight to the consumer mentality that remains an American staple today. Products produced by skilled labor rely on a large profit margin from a limited number of products. Mass production relies on a small profit margin across a large number of products. Thus, instead of selling one expensive watch, companies began to mass-produce watches, which required them to sell large numbers of them at a reduced markup. In effect, it made watches and other products affordable to a larger number of people. To keep employees in unskilled assembly-line jobs, which were repetitive and boring for many workers, Henry Ford paid his workers around five dollars a day at a time when the going rate for unskilled labor was around two dollars a day. This not only meant more income for unskilled workers, it meant more customers for the products that were being mass-produced.

Mass production and its accompanying advertising helped create an increased interest in material goods—in having and acquiring *things*. This attitude is evident in *The Great Gatsby*. It can be found in the character of Myrtle Wilson, Tom Buchanan's mistress, who is preoccupied with the things that Tom can buy for her.

The Distribution of Wealth

As America became a modern industrialized nation at the end of the nineteenth and the beginning of the twentieth centuries, the families who owned the factories began to accumulate a great deal of wealth. By the end of the 1920s, nearly half of the nation's wealth was owned by only one percent of the population, which created a large gap between America's wealthiest and poorest citizens. "Industrial princes" lived lives of opulence while immigrant workers lived lives of degradation.

Nowhere in Fitzgerald's work is this class distinction more graphically depicted than in *The Great Gatsby*. Fitzgerald contrasts the opulent lifestyles of people in East and West Egg with the desolate landscape of the valley of ashes where George Wilson struggles to make a life for himself, only to have that life destroyed by the carelessness of the wealthy people who merely pass by on their way to the city.

Prohibition and Gangsters

On January 16, 1919, the Eighteenth Amendment to the U.S. Constitution was ratified, making illegal the manufacture, sale, and transportation of alcohol in the United States.

THE EIGHTEENTH AMENDMENT TO THE U.S. CONSTITUTION

Section 1. After one year from the ratification of this article the manufacture, sale, or transportation of intoxicating liquors within, the importation thereof into, or the exportation thereof from the United States and all territory subject to the jurisdiction thereof for beverage purposes is hereby prohibited.

Section 2. The Congress and the several States shall have concurrent power to enforce this article by appropriate legislation.

Section 3. This article shall be inoperative unless it shall have been ratified as an amendment to the Constitution by the legislatures of the several States, as provided in the Constitution, within seven years from the date of the submission hereof to the States by the Congress.

The Amendment went into effect on January 16, 1920. Although making alcohol illegal resulted in an initial reduction in drinking, it also opened the doors to a very profitable criminal enterprise: bootlegging.

Unable to buy alcohol legally, people turned to bootleggers, who smuggled alcohol across Canadian and Mexican borders. Criminal organizations also took over the manufacture of alcohol. Because Prohibition booze was illegal, there were risks involved in its manufacture and delivery. This made the cost of alcohol soar, increasing its profitability to criminals. The fact that the income from the sale of alcohol was tax free increased its profitability.

Crime syndicates sprang up in urban areas to supply illegal drinking establishments, known as "speakeasies," with alcohol. Al Capone was one of the most notorious crime leaders. His income for 1929 has been estimated at over $100 million (equivalent to about $1.5 billion today), 60 percent of which came directly from trafficking in illegal alcohol.

The huge profits criminals garnered from bootlegging enabled them to pay off political officials, police, and key members of the legal community (Kallen 2002, 101). The result was free-flowing booze and vicious gang wars with very little legal interference. One owner of a New York City speakeasy recounts: "We would slip the captain a $50 bill from time to time and a box of cigars to the cops on the beat. They could always count on us for free meals and drinks, and at Christmas time, of course, we had a gift for everybody" (See Kallen 2002, 101).

Alcohol figures prominently in F. Scott Fitzgerald's works. In *The Great Gatsby*, people suspect Jay Gatsby of earning his money as a bootlegger, which makes him a notorious criminal and an object of fascination for members of the upper social classes. Alcohol also figured in Fitzgerald's life. At the beginning of his career, he avoided

FEDERAL AGENTS DESTROYING BARRELS OF ALCOHOL DURING PROHIBITION.

drinking when he wrote; toward the end of his career, he was unable to write unless he drank.

In 1922, Fitzgerald said the following about Prohibition and its impact on drinking in New York City:

> [N]ight life . . . [i]s going on as it never was before Prohibition. I'm confident that you can find anything here that you find in Paris. Everybody is drinking harder— that's sure. Possessing liquor is a proof of respectability, of social position. You can't go anywhere without having your host bring out his bottle and offer you a drink. He displays his liquor as he used to display his new car or his wife's jewels. (Bruccoli and Baughman 2004, 26)

Electricity, Radio, and the Telephone

The first part of the twentieth century was a period of rapid changes in American culture. Fitzgerald's works helped capture those changes, incorporating the proliferation of electronic devices and the telephone into the atmosphere of his novels and stories. In 1907 only 8 percent of American households had electricity, but by 1920 this had increased to 35 percent. By 1939, 80 percent of America had electricity.

Along with the home wiring came new, affordable radios. Corporations such as RCA and Westinghouse began to broadcast scheduled programming. The National Broadcast Company (NBC) was formed in 1926, and the Columbia Broadcasting System (CBS) was organized in 1928. Radio, along with the phonograph and motion pictures, helped to unify American thought. People in one part of the country were exposed to the same images and ideas as people in another part of the country. Someone on the West Coast could buy a dress from a store, catch a movie at the theater, drive home in his or her automobile, and listen to a radio program, while someone on the East Coast bought the exact same dress, watched the same movie, drove home in an identical automobile, and listened to the same program on the same model of radio.

Automobiles and Travel

Between 1907 and 1928, automobile production in America increased from 45,000 new automobiles a year to more than 4 million, making America the leading manufacturer of automobiles in the world. By the end of the 1920s, one in every five people in America owned a car.

Americans were now able to move more freely about the country, and did not have to live close to stores and the workplace. They could drive to the store to stock up on merchandise. This new freedom contributed to the growth of suburbs and an increase in middle-class consumers. It also contributed to a freer lifestyle for young Americans, as Frederick Lewis Allen, editor of *The Atlantic Monthly* and *Harper's*, noted in a 1931 essay:

> A new sort of freedom was being made possible by the enormous increase in the use of the automobile, and particularly of the closed car. (In 1919 hardly more than 10 per cent of the cars produced in the United States were closed; by 1924 the percentage had jumped to 43, by 1927 it had reached 82.8.) The automobile offered an almost universally available means of escaping temporarily from the supervision of parents and chaperons, or from the influence of neighborhood opinion. Boys and girls now thought nothing . . . of jumping into a car and driving off at a moment's notice—without asking anybody's permission—to a dance in another town twenty miles away, where they were strangers and enjoyed a freedom impossible among their neighbors. (Kallen 2002, 139–140)

The automobile became an American symbol of freedom and status. It often figures into F. Scott Fitzgerald's writing. In the short story, "Winter Dreams," the liberating effect of the automobile Allen notes above is evident. Judy re-establishes her romantic hold on Dexter in the privacy of his coupe. Fitzgerald writes:

> In then, with a rustle of golden cloth. He slammed the door. Into so many cars she

had stepped—like this—like that—her back against the leather, so—her elbow resting on the door—waiting. . . . With an effort he forced himself to start the car and back into the street. This was nothing, he must remember. She had done this before. (Fitzgerald 1989, 231)

In *The Great Gatsby*, Tom Buchanan uses his blue coupe to manipulate his mistress's husband, George Wilson. For Wilson, the coupe represents an opportunity to earn money and build a better life for himself and his wife. It symbolizes the American Dream. Gatsby's big, yellow car is a sign of his status. His Rolls Royce, like his mansion, reflects his success.

Fitzgerald uses the automobile to reveal flaws in the American Dream. Buchanan has no intention of selling his coupe to Wilson. To do so would be to lose his leverage over the man. Thus, the car symbolizes the prosperity that Buchanan possesses and Wilson will never achieve.

The fact that an accident with Gatsby's car marks the tragic turning point in *The Great Gatsby* is an example of the centrality of the automobile to American consciousness in the 1920s.

Flappers and the New Woman

The term "flapper" originated in England during the nineteenth century, where it described an "immoral young girl" (Oxford English Dictionary 2004). In America during the first part of the twentieth century, the term referred to a combination of lifestyle, fashion, and attitude found in some young women during the 1920s. The flapper symbolized a new age in America, one in which women faced fewer restrictions. Flapper fashion was also less restrictive: loose-fitting and more revealing dresses, raised hemlines,

FLAPPERS CHALLENGED THE CONVENTIONS OF THE TIME. ABOVE,
TWO FLAPPERS DANCE ON TOP OF A BUILDING LEDGE.

exposed stockings, long scarves, quirky hats, short hair, and makeup (primarily rouge and lipstick). The flapper way of life was a marked departure from the confining mores that kept young girls' mothers wrapped in corsets and trapped at home. The flapper smoked in public, applied makeup at the dinner table, drank, and made out at dance parties. Sex was more openly discussed, at least in part due to Sigmund Freud and the pervasive influence of his "science" of psychology over Western thought.

One interviewer, attributing Fitzgerald's "flapper" to Zelda, summarized Zelda's attitudes in defining the term in a 1923 interview for the Louisville *Courier-Journal*:

> [I]s she [Zelda] the living prototype of that species of femininity known as the American flapper? If so, what is a flapper like in real life? Here is a tabloid account of Zelda Fitzgerald:
>
> Flappers. She likes them reckless and unconventional, because of their quest in search of self-expression.
>
> Sports. Golf and swimming.
>
> Jazz music, "because it is artistic," and dancing for its sheer abandon. Not ambitious to be a "joiner"—just enjoy life to the full. Large families "so children have a chance to be what they want to be." Wants her own daughter to be "rich, happy and artistic." (Bruccoli and Baughman 2004, 46)

But there was more to women in the 1920s than dance marathons and risqué behavior. On August 18, 1920, the Nineteenth Amendment to the U.S. Constitution was rat-

Dance marathons (also known as Walkathons, "bunion derbies," and "corn and cal'lus carnivals") were a popular fad that sprang up in the 1920s. These endurance contests drew large crowds and sometimes lasted as long as two months.

ified. For the first time in the history of America, women had the right to vote. During World War I, women had entered the workforce to fill positions formerly reserved for men. Charles Panati believed women took on the persona of the flapper as a way to gain power. He wrote:

> [The Flapper] gained entry into the impenetrable male world in the guise of a

"boy"—a tomboy—where she played at "men's" behaviors—smoking and drinking and keeping the wee hours—all the while staking out a territory and power base that, when she dropped the flat-chested guise to go back to full bosom frills, men would never quite win back. On the battlefield of the sexes, the flapper was women's Trojan horse. (Panati, 116–117)

The 1920s was the first decade of liberation for women, resulting from feminist efforts begun at Seneca Falls in 1848. Women had come a long way and worked hard to achieve some control over their own destinies. The attitudes of young women in the 1920s were partially a result of that first flush of freedom for modern American women. They had more independence than their mothers had. They could decide for themselves what they would wear, where they would go, what they would do, and with whom they would do it.

THE NINETEENTH AMENDMENT TO THE U.S. CONSTITUTION

The right of citizens of the United States to vote shall not be denied or abridged by the United States or by any State on account of sex.

Congress shall have power to enforce this article by appropriate legislation.

Expatriates and the Lost Generation

The terms "expatriate" and "Lost Generation" are frequent in discussions of the 1920s. They are important to understand because F. Scott Fitzgerald's name is associated with both—he is considered by many to be one of the expatriates who moved to France in the 1920s, and a charter member of the Lost Generation.

An expatriate is a person who voluntarily lives outside his or her country. By this definition, the term is accurate when applied to Fitzgerald, Hemingway, Langston Hughes, and other American writers who traveled to Europe in the 1920s. But Fitzgerald remained quintessentially American even though he traveled to Europe several times in his life and socialized with other writers and artists living in and around Paris.

Fitzgerald was more representative of American attitudes during the 1920s in that he went to Europe for a change of scenery. Europe had been the primary battleground of the largest military conflict in the history of the world (WWI), and many traveled there out of a sense of adventure.

"The Lost Generation" is a term coined by the writer Gertrude Stein. Although it is often used in connection with expatriate writers and artists in Paris during the 1920s, the term, as Marc Dolan points out, is "difficult to classify." Dolan writes:

> Who or what was "the lost generation"? In a way, it depended on who was talking about it. At various times and in various mouths and hands, those three bare words referred to: a literal group of coevals (women and men born at approximately the same time); a specific cultural subset of that demographic grouping; a theory of how American arts, letters, and culture evolved in the years following World War I; and a complex of mythic tropes, characters, and settings that enshrined the memory of an early twentieth century that almost certainly never existed. (Dolan 1996, 9)

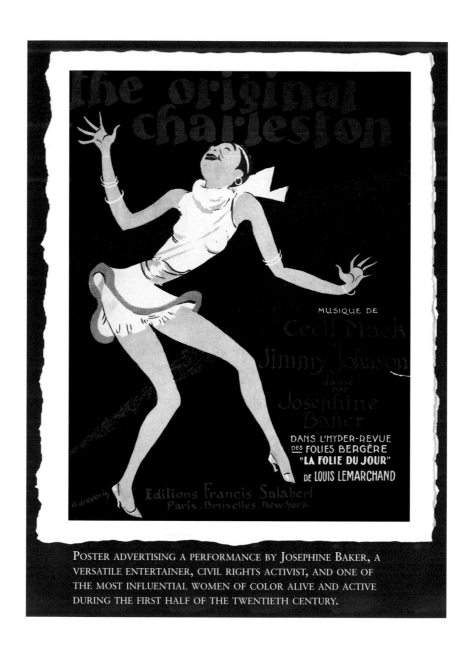

POSTER ADVERTISING A PERFORMANCE BY JOSEPHINE BAKER, A VERSATILE ENTERTAINER, CIVIL RIGHTS ACTIVIST, AND ONE OF THE MOST INFLUENTIAL WOMEN OF COLOR ALIVE AND ACTIVE DURING THE FIRST HALF OF THE TWENTIETH CENTURY.

The term "Lost Generation" generally refers to a dissatisfaction among young people in the 1920s—a longing for something meaningful in their lives, something they did not feel they could find by remaining where they were.

Both "expatriate" and "the Lost Generation" say more about the way critics, scholars, and others choose to imagine a period in the history of America than how that period actually was. Some people moved to Europe to get away from America, such as African-American entertainer Josephine Baker, who moved to Paris to escape racism in America. But many American writers and artists moved to Europe for other reasons—some were merely curious, and some, such as the Fitzgeralds, went partly because the favorable currency exchange rates increased the buying power of their money.

Fitzgerald was an expatriate because he spent time out of the country and he was a member of the Lost Generation in that he represented a particular type of American who had attempted to cast off established values.

exhaustible charm that rose and fell in it, the jingle of
ughter, the golden girl. . ."Her voice is full of money," he
ll of money—that was the inexhaustible charm that rose a
a white palace the king's daughter, the golden girl. . ."H
derstood it before. It was full of money—that was the ine
mbals' song of it. . . . High in a white palace the king's
ddenly. That was it. I'd never understood it before. It wa
ll in it, the jingle of it, the cymbals' song of it. . . . Hi
ce is full of money," he said suddenly. That was it. I'd ne
ustible charm that rose and fell in it, the jingle of it
ughter, the golden girl. . ."Her voice is full of money," he
ll of money—that was the inexhaustible charm that rose a
a white palace the king's daughter, the golden girl. . ."H
derstood it before. It was full of money—that was the in
mbals' song of it. . . . High in a white palace the king's
ddenly. That was it. I'd never understood it before. It w
ll in it, the jingle of it, the cymbals' song of it. . . . Hi
ce is full of money," he said suddenly. That was it. I'd n
ustible charm that rose and fell in it, the jingle of i
ughter, the golden girl. . ."Her voice is full of money," he
ll of money—that was the inexhaustible charm that rose a
a white palace the king's daughter, the golden girl. . ."H
derstood it before. It was full of money—that was the in
mbals' song of it. . . . High in a white palace the king's
ddenly. That was it. I'd never understood it before. It w
ll in it, the jingle of it, the cymbals' song of it. . . . Hi
ce is full of money," he said suddenly. That was it. I'd n
ustible charm that rose and fell in it, the jingle of i
ughter, the golden girl. . ."Her voice is full of money," he
ll of money—that was the inexhaustible charm that rose
a white palace the king's daughter, the golden girl. . ."H
derstood it before. It was full of money—that was the in
mbals' song of it. . . . High in a white palace the king's
ddenly. That was it. I'd never understood it before. It w
ll in it, the jingle of it, the cymbals' song of it. . . . H
ce is full of money," he said suddenly. That was it. I'd n
ustible charm that rose and fell in it, the jingle of i

Part II:
The Writing of
F. Scott Fitzgerald

Introduction

F. SCOTT FITZGERALD'S NAME FIRST APPEARED in print at the age of thirteen when he published a short story, "The Mystery of the Raymond Mortgage," in St. Paul Academy's *Now and Then*. His first literary sale was a poem (written while he was attending Princeton), which the magazine *Poet Lore* paid him for but never published (Turnbull, *Biography*, p. 78). The work that marks the beginning of his professional career is "Porcelain and Pink (A One-Act Play)," which was published in January 1920 in *The Smart Set*, a popular magazine of the time.

> An author ought to write for the youth of his generation, the critics of the next, and the schoolmasters of ever afterward.
> —F. Scott Fitzgerald

Throughout his life, Fitzgerald wrote poetry, plays, song lyrics, screenplays, short stories, essays, and novels, but it is his short stories and novels that have earned him a high place in literary history. Fitzgerald published about 160 stories (many included in four book-length short-story collections) and four novels during his career. A fifth novel, *The Last Tycoon*, was never completed, but the unfinished manuscript was published the year after he died.

Fitzgerald's works vary in quality, but most readers agree that his best work was his novel *The Great Gatsby*. *Gatsby* is the work for which he is best known, although his short stories earned him early fortune and fame.

Andrew Turnbull recounts that when Fitzgerald was still in college at Princeton he told a professor that "he thought it in his power to write either books that would sell or books of permanent value, and he wasn't sure which he should do" (1962, 62). Fitzgerald wrestled with this issue throughout his career, longing to write great fiction while dependent on the easy money that his more popular, but less literary, efforts earned.

The greatness of a work depends a lot on who is reading it. Different readers tend to value different characteristics. In broad terms, readers tend to look at an author's ability to effectively and poetically use language, his or her ability to create believable characters, and his or her ability to construct an engaging plot. Readers often rate a work based on how well it meets those criteria. Because readers of popular fiction tend to value plot over character and language, they may favorably judge a novel with weak characterizations and poor use of language if it has an engaging plot. H. L. Mencken's claim that *The Great Gatsby* failed to get "under the skin of its people" (Mizener 1974, 169) implies a weak use of character. Mencken's admission that he is impressed by "the charm and beauty of the writing" (Mizener 1974, 169) refers to Fitzgerald's use of language.

Although some of Fitzgerald's work may be judged harshly on plot, and a smaller percentage on character, even his least successful stories always possessed a spark of brilliance in his use of language.

THE GREAT GATSBY HAS BEEN FILMED SEVERAL TIMES; PERHAPS THE VERSION BEST KNOWN TO AMERICAN AUDIENCES IS THE 1974 FILM STARRING ROBERT REDFORD AND MIA FARROW.

Chapter 1

The Great Gatsby
Background on the
Writing of The Great Gatsby

F. Scott Fitzgerald worked on *The Great Gatsby* at Villa Marie, Valescure, St. Raphaël, in France during the summer and fall of 1924 (Bruccoli, Smith, & Kerr 2003, 116). He rewrote the proofs at the Hôtel des Princes in Rome in the winter of 1924–1925. The book was published on April 10, 1925.

Several short stories, such as "Winter Dreams," "Absolution," "The Sensible Thing," "The Diamond as Big as the Ritz," "Dice, Brass Knuckles & Guitar" (Bruccoli 1995, viii; Flanagan 2000), and "The Rich Boy" contain glimpses of characters and themes found in *The Great Gatsby.* "Absolution" was to have been the prologue of *The Great Gatsby,* but Fitzgerald felt it "interfered with the neatness of the plan" (Turnbull 1963, 164). According to Matthew J. Bruccoli, *The Great Gatsby* had a "three-year process of evolution" and achieved "its ultimate brilliance when Fitzgerald revised and rewrote it in the galley proofs" (Bruccoli 1995, viii–ix).

It is clear from letters Fitzgerald wrote while working on *The Great Gatsby* that he was aware that the novel represented a step forward for him as an author. In April of 1924, he wrote to his editor, Maxwell Perkins, and said:

> [I]n my new novel I'm thrown directly on purely creative work—not trashy imaginings as in my stories but the sustained imagination of a sincere yet radiant world. So I tread slowly and carefully and at

times in considerable distress. This book will be a consciously artistic achievement and must depend on that as the first books did not. (Turnbull 1963, 163)

Fitzgerald considered *The Great Gatsby* his chance to "start over" (Turnbull 1963, 168) and even refused to have blurbs on the book jacket because he knew they would refer to him as the author of *This Side of Paradise*.

The Great Gatsby represents Fitzgerald at his best. He labored over the manuscript. He struggled with its title. Several he considered were "Gold-hatted Gatsby," "Trimalchio," "On the Road to West Egg," and "The High-bouncing Lover." At the last minute, he tried to change the title to "Under the Red, White, and Blue," but the book had already gone to press, and it was too late to make changes.

Andrew Hook argues that "the key to *The Great Gatsby*'s success as a novel—and the reason why it does represent a major advance in Fitzgerald's art of fiction—lies in its form, and its narrative form in particular." Both of Fitzgerald's previous novels, Hook claims, "suffer from Fitzgerald's uneven control of narrative structure. . . . [while] The consistent use of Nick Carraway as an internal narrator [in *Gatsby*] imposes a new kind of narrative discipline on *The Great Gatsby*: the result is a satisfying sense of formal unity and coherence" (Hook 1992, 48).

Principal Characters in *The Great Gatsby*

Daisy Fay Buchanan

Daisy Buchanan is Nick Carraway's cousin. She is from a well-to-do family in Louisville, Kentucky. She and Jay Gatsby fell in love years before the novel takes place, when Gatsby was an army officer in Louisville. When the military sent Gatsby away, Daisy promised to wait for his return, but she eventually grew tired of waiting and married Tom Buchanan, a wealthy society figure. During the course of the novel, Daisy lives with her husband and their three-year-old daughter in East Egg, a section of Long Island reserved for old money.

Daisy serves several key functions. For one, she is the object of Gatsby's obsessive love, the reason he has come to Long Island, and his primary motivation for becoming wealthy. He throws lavish parties for the purpose of attracting as a guest someone who knows Daisy or Daisy herself.

For another, Daisy is emblematic of the social upper classes. Fitzgerald's novel implies that Daisy's social position may have more to do with Gatsby's passion for her than Gatsby realizes. As a full-fledged member of the wealthy upper class, Daisy, like her husband Tom, is careless with the hearts and lives of others. Fitzgerald leads readers to question whether or not it was her wealth and social standing that resulted in her careless, childlike nature.

Tom Buchanan

Tom Buchanan is Daisy's husband and was a Yale classmate of Nick Carraway's. A former university athlete, Tom is well-built, but of limited intellectual ability, as well as being intensely racist and sexist. He comes from an extremely wealthy family and values his possessions. He considers Daisy one of his possessions. During the time of the story, Tom keeps a mistress (Myrtle Wilson).

Fitzgerald's portrait of Tom is of a cruel and insensitive man full of lost potential. He was a football hero in college, yet his life is one of self-indulgence, immorality, and callousness. His great wealth cushions him against the world. Tom and Daisy are of the same world, the world the narrator, Nick Carraway, ultimately turns his back on.

Tom is considered by many (including Fitzgerald) to be Fitzgerald's most fully realized character.

Jordan Baker

Jordan Baker is an amateur golfer. She is Daisy's friend and Nick Carraway's casual love interest. Jordan parallels Daisy. The fact that she cheats at golf reflects the decay of morality during the 1920s, a theme that courses through the entire novel. On the surface, Nick finds her appealing, yet beneath her exterior lies the same trivial, careless nature we find in Tom and Daisy Buchanan. Nick's rejection of her at the end of the novel parallels his rejection of the East and is part of his decision to head home to the Midwest.

Nick Carraway

Nick Carraway narrates the story, so everything in the novel is colored by his perception. At the start of the novel, he is a twenty-nine-year-old man (he turns thirty during the course of the story), a graduate of Yale University, like Tom Buchanan, and a veteran of World War I (then called the Great War). Nick is from the Midwest, but the story he relates is about a time when he was living in West Egg, a section of Long Island, New York (based on the Hamptons), where the newly rich live. Nick is Daisy Buchanan's cousin.

Although he chronicles Jay Gatsby's story, Nick's life resonates throughout the novel. Like Gatsby, Nick is full of hope. Like Gatsby, Nick sees those hopes dashed by the harsh reality of the world. Gatsby believes he only needs to regain Daisy to achieve the fulfillment of his life's ambition and escape his humble beginnings. In observing Gatsby's pursuit of Daisy and Gatsby's ultimate failure, Nick learns that the lifestyles of the wealthy upper classes, though they appear enchanting, are actually rife with self-indulgence, waste, and conspicuous consumption.

Jay Gatsby (James Gatz)

Jay Gatsby is the title character. He is first seen as a mysterious character with a seemingly endless flow of money. He lives in a huge mansion in West Egg (next door to Nick Carraway's bungalow), where he frequently throws extravagant parties. During the course of the novel, we learn that Jay Gatsby was born James Gatz, a North Dakota farm boy. While in Louisville, Kentucky, training to be an officer, he meets and falls in love with Daisy. Through illegal activities he manages to accumulate in a short period of time a large fortune that he hopes will allow him to fit into Daisy's world and win her back.

Gatsby is controlled by his longing for Daisy and destroyed by his inability to break free of his past. She is no longer the woman he knew, yet he is unable to see her for who she is because that would contradict the myth that has shaped his life—the dream that promises everything to a man who persists toward his goals. Gatsby's unyielding pursuit of Daisy leads to his tragic end.

Henry C. Gatz

Jay Gatsby's father appears at the end of the novel and provides Nick with insight into Gatsby's character. Gatz's entrance into the novel reveals Gatsby's past, exposing his humble beginnings and showing how far he had come to escape the life into which he was born.

George Wilson

A simple, poor owner of a gas station and repair shop in the "valley of ashes," a desolate area of land halfway between

West Egg and New York City, covered in industrial ash. George is married to Myrtle Wilson, with whom Tom is having an affair.

George Wilson is Tom Buchanan's opposite, a man with little education, little money, no social standing, and little hope for the future. Wilson's life symbolizes the futility of the working class, who live in the wastelands created by industry.

Myrtle Wilson

Myrtle is a vulgar, sensuous woman in her midthirties. She feels trapped by her marriage to George Wilson. Myrtle mistakenly views her affair with Tom Buchanan, a man who is wealthy beyond her imaginings, as a way to change her lot in life.

Myrtle's longing for Tom is based on his ability to buy things and represents the desire for possessions and misplaced values of the 1920s in America. Her hopes, like her husband's, rest on Tom Buchanan who remains indifferent to George and casually amused by Myrtle.

Meyer Wolfshiem

Meyer Wolfshiem is a criminal for whom Gatsby works. Wolfshiem was responsible for fixing the 1919 World Series. Wolfshiem serves two functions in *The Great Gatsby*: First, he casts a shadow over Gatsby's character. From Gatsby's dealings with Wolfshiem we learn that Gatsby's wealth flows to him through illegal channels. Second, Wolfshiem symbolizes the erosion of ethics in America during the first part of the twentieth century.

Overview of *The Great Gatsby*

Chapter I

The Great Gatsby is narrated by Nick Carraway. At the opening of the novel, Nick describes his nature as one of reserved judgment. He believes this makes him "privy to the secret griefs of wild, unknown men" (Fitzgerald 1968, 3). [All citations to *The Great Gatsby* are to this edition.]

We know from the beginning that Nick's encounter with Gatsby has changed Nick. Nick tells us that after his experiences with Gatsby and the East he "wanted no more riotous excursions with privileged glimpses into the human heart" (4). Thus the novel begins with a question about the nature of Nick's disillusionment.

> Fitzgerald makes it quite clear that Gatsby chooses to be shackled to Daisy, to be incarnate, to cut himself off from the inspiration of a celestial note. From the boundless freedom of a wider universe he turns to the narrower world where mortal beauty is the inspirational factor.
> (Chambers 1989, 98–99)

Several of the novel's main themes appear in the first chapter:

The Decay of the American Dream

Nick has traveled to the East to find his place for himself away from family pressures. He is seeking the American Dream. Gatsby also seeks the American Dream and so Gatsby's fate and Nick's revelation reflect the status of the American Dream in the first part of the twentieth century.

Class and Social Standing

Distinctions between new money and old money are outlined symbolically in the differences between East and West Egg. These two communities symbolize American distinctions between the East Coast and West Coast. The East Coast, being the older, more established region of the country, is represented by East Egg, the more fashionable community. The West Coast, which has long symbolized the American frontier, is represented by West Egg, the home of the *nouveau riche*. But class in the novel is even more fully expressed as each character is firmly rooted in his or her social standing. In the first chapter we are introduced to the upper class to which Tom and Daisy Buchanan belong and to which Nick is related. By the close of the novel, we encounter many other classes, such as the *nouveau riche* of West Egg, the poor, working class who live in the valley of ashes, and the criminal class to which Wolfshiem belongs.

The Immorality of the Age
Much of *The Great Gatsby* exposes the reduced morality of the period in American history during which it takes place. This is evident from the dinner party in the first chapter where Nick learns that Tom is having an affair. Despite Tom and Daisy's wealth and superficial gaiety, it is obvious to Nick that there are problems below the glimmering surface of their lives.

> For a moment the last sunshine fell with romantic affection upon her glowing face; her voice compelled me forward breathlessly as I listened—then the glow faded, each light deserting her with lingering regret, like children leaving a pleasant street at dusk.
> *The Great Gatsby* (20)

The first chapter ends with Nick's first sighting of Gatsby, whom he spies staring out across the bay at a single green dock light on the other side. The light, which we later learn is on the dock at Daisy's mansion in East Egg, is a significant symbol in the novel. It represents the past which Gatsby longs to regain—his days in Louisville with Daisy. In that single light, all of Gatsby's hopes and dreams are invested. He is transfixed by it, just as he is possessed by his past relationship with Daisy.

Chapter II

Two important symbols are introduced in Chapter II. First, we are shown the "valley of ashes," a desolate area halfway between West Egg and New York City. The stark imagery of the valley of ashes contrasts the wealth of East and West Egg. Its landscape is covered with factory ash. A small, polluted river runs along one side of the valley. This is a wasteland created by the very industries that maintain the wealthy residents of East Egg and New York City.

Second, we see for the first time the large advertisement for an optometrist that overlooks the valley of ashes, with its giant blue eyes and "enormous yellow spectacles" (31)—the "eyes of Doctor T. J. Eckleburg" (30). Some critics argue that the eyes symbolize that God is dead. Eckleburg oversees the careless actions of the wealthy—Tom's affair with Myrtle, the automobile accident, Tom's abuse of George, and so on—yet no judgment is made on the people who commit these acts. No divine force intervenes to correct the injustice we witness. Another way to view Eckleburg's eyes is as a symbol for the objective view of the reader, who is above the action and who must determine for him or herself how to judge these characters in the novel.

The impromptu gathering in New York City that constitutes the bulk of Chapter II contrasts with the dinner party in Chapter I. While the party in Chapter I reveals the superficial lives of the wealthy upper class, the gathering in

Chapter II introduces us to the lower class's sensibilities. Myrtle's behavior is particularly important here. In acting the role of the socialite, she exposes her lower-class upbringing. Her pathetic mimicry of elitist behaviors starkly contrasts with Daisy's behavior. Daisy has the life Myrtle desires, but it is evident in Chapter II that Myrtle would never fit into Tom Buchanan's world, and that he is associating with Myrtle and her group for idle amusement—to stave off the boredom of his social standing.

> People disappeared, reappeared, made plans to go somewhere, and then lost each other, searched for each other, found each other a few feet away. Sometime toward midnight Tom Buchanan and Mrs. Wilson stood face to face, discussing in impassioned voices whether Mrs. Wilson had any right to mention Daisy's name.
>
> "Daisy! Daisy! Daisy!" shouted Mrs. Wilson. I'll say it whenever I want to! Daisy! Dai—"
>
> Making a short deft movement, Tom Buchanan broke her nose with his open hand.
> *The Great Gatsby* (47–48)

The people at Tom and Myrtle's party gossip about Gatsby just as the people at Tom and Daisy's party gossiped about Gatsby, helping define Gatsby as someone familiar to both social circles, but known by neither.

Chapter III
Chapter III presents us with the third party. This time Nick describes in detail Gatsby's parties, which are lavish,

excessive, and frequent. Here, as before, rumors about Gatsby abound, and in the wide variety of characters who attend the party we find a blending of classes. Members of the Buchanan's social circle and members of Myrtle's social circle are in attendance.

Nick and Gatsby's meeting in this chapter begins their relationship, which is based primarily on Gatsby's desire to locate someone who knows Daisy. Nick and Gatsby both served in the war and are therefore both members of that group of disillusioned veterans who suffered its brutalities only to return to a country caught up in political hypocrisy, rampant materialism, and the desire for quick money.

Nick and Gatsby also share the desire to create some sense of stability in their lives, Nick by pursuing a career in bond trading, and Gatsby by regaining his past love with Daisy.

The mystery of Gatsby is intensified when Jordan Baker emerges from her private meeting with him and claims to have "just heard the most amazing thing" (67), which she promised not to repeat.

In the last part of the chapter, Nick reminds us that he has been working on learning the bond business and seeing Jordan, whom he has learned is "incurably dishonest" (75). In the end, he recounts the following argument he had with Jordan about her driving:

> "You're a rotten driver," I protested.
> "Either you ought to be more careful, or
> you oughtn't to drive at all."
> "I am careful."
> "No, you're not."
> "Well, other people are," she said lightly.
> "What's that got to do with it?"
> "They'll keep out of my way," she insisted.

"It takes two to make an accident."
"Suppose you met somebody just as careless as yourself."

"I hope I never will," she answered. "I
hate careless people. That's why I like
you." (75)

This particular exchange foreshadows what we learn
about Daisy and Tom by the end of the novel—that they
are two careless people and that their carelessness leads to
tragedy for those unfortunate enough to cross their path.

Chapter IV
Chapter IV begins with a list of people Nick recalls seeing
at Gatsby's parties. This list further builds the sense that
Gatsby's parties included people from a broad range of
classes, professions, and backgrounds.

Then it was all true. I saw the skins of
tigers flaming in his palace on the Grand
Canal; I saw him opening a chest of rubies
to ease, with their crimson-lighted depths,
the gnawing of his broken heart.
The Great Gatsby (85)

Several key pieces of the puzzle now appear. We learn
of Gatsby's early relationship with Daisy and how Daisy
reluctantly married Tom. We discover that Tom has been
unfaithful to Daisy from the beginning of their marriage.
We discover that on the night of the party in the previous
chapter, Gatsby asked Jordan Baker about Nick and that
Gatsby wants Nick to set up a meeting between Gatsby
and Daisy.

Chapter IV also provides us with our first clue to the
darker side of Gatsby's personality, when Nick and

Gatsby lunch with Meyer Wolfshiem. Wolfshiem, who fixed the 1919 World Series, is Gatsby's boss. Gatsby's affiliation with him lends credibility to the rumors that Gatsby earned his wealth as a bootlegger.

Chapter V
In Chapter V, Gatsby and Daisy are reunited. It is important to note that this meeting takes place in the middle of the novel. The first four chapters cover events leading up to Gatsby and Daisy's meeting and the final four chapters cover events occurring after the two are brought back together. Fitzgerald uses weather imagery during this section. It is raining heavily before Gatsby and Daisy meet at Nick's for tea, but as their relationship re-forms, the rain dissipates and the sun re-emerges.

> There must have been moments even that afternoon when Daisy tumbled short of his dreams—not through her own fault, but because of the colossal vitality of his illusion. It had gone beyond her, beyond everything. He had thrown himself into it with a creative passion, adding to it all the time, decking it out with every bright feather that drifted his way. No amount of fire or freshness can challenge what a man will store up in his ghostly heart.
> *The Great Gatsby* (121–122)

As Gatsby, Daisy, and Nick tour Gatsby's mansion, it becomes clear to Nick, if to no one else, that Daisy has changed in the five years since her first romantic encounters with Gatsby. The romantic moment is haunted by changes in Daisy's character and the first hints that all the elements of Gatsby's life (his wealth, his possessions, and his feelings for Daisy) are based on an illusion. Gatsby believes that through the force of his will he can make time retreat to an earlier day by eliminating all that has happened since he and Daisy first said good-bye. Like Nick, we begin to realize that the Daisy of five years earlier, whom Gatsby loves so deeply, is not the Daisy Buchanan of today, but a creation of Gatsby's imagination.

Chapter VI
At the start of Chapter VI, Nick unfolds the truth about Gatsby's background, and we learn just how far Gatsby has come, from his beginning as the son of "shiftless and unsuccessful farm people" (124) to his present wealth.

> He wanted nothing less of Daisy than that she should go to Tom and say: "I never loved you." After she had obliterated four years with that sentence they could decide upon the more practical measures to be taken. One of them was that, after she was free, they were to go back to Louisville and be married from her house—just as if it were five years ago.
>
> *The Great Gatsby* (139)

The remainder of the chapter covers two incidents at Gatsby's mansion. In the first, Tom Buchanan shows up there. Gatsby is curious about Tom and admits that he knows Tom's wife, a confession that Tom finds merely curious. When Gatsby is invited to dinner by one of Tom's friends, Gatsby accepts in what is understood by readers as a breach of social protocol. Tom and his two friends leave while Gatsby is retrieving his coat.

The second incident involves the first time Tom and Daisy attend one of Gatsby's parties. Fitzgerald presents a series of scenes involving Tom and Daisy and the other guests at the party. Gatsby's parties, despite their lavish expense, seem gauche. Nick tells us that Daisy is "appalled by West Egg . . . appalled by its raw vigor that chafed under the old euphemisms and by the too obtrusive fate that herded its inhabitants along a short cut from nothing to nothing" (136). Both incidents imply that Gatsby's great wealth and luxurious surroundings cannot buy his way into the upper classes.

At Gatsby's request, Nick stays until all the other guests have left or gone to bed. Gatsby confesses to Nick that something is different about Daisy. She is unable to live up to the ideal Gatsby has fashioned over the past five years. Nevertheless, Gatsby is confident that he can "fix everything just the way it was before" (140).

Chapter VII
The climax of the novel occurs in Chapter VII during another party. The party at Tom and Daisy's house invites a comparison to the party that begins the novel. Everyone present at the first party is also at this party, but this time Gatsby is also there. He is an intrusive outsider and disrupts the casual boredom of the upper-class group, as Tom makes clear by insulting Gatsby's social status. "I'll be damned if I see how you got within a mile of her unless you brought the groceries to the back door" (165), Tom says. He refers to Gatsby as "Mr. Nobody from Nowhere" (163).

This chapter presents revelations and confusion. Tom learns of Daisy's relationship with Gatsby. George Wilson learns of Myrtle's affair. Tom exposes Gatsby's illicit business practices by pointing out Gatsby's relationship with Meyer

Wolfshiem. Daisy learns where Gatsby gets his money. Gatsby learns that Daisy does love Tom.

> "Who wants to go to town?" demanded Daisy insistently. Gatsby's eyes floated toward her. "Ah," she cried, "you look so cool."
>
> Their eyes met, and they stared together at each other, alone in space. With an effort she glanced down at the table.
>
> "You always look so cool," she repeated. She had told him that she loved him, and Tom Buchanan saw. He was astounded. His mouth opened a little, and he looked at Gatsby, and then back at Daisy as if he had just recognized her as someone he knew a long time ago.
>
> *The Great Gatsby* (149–150)

Ironically, rather than clarifying matters, these revelations create confusion, as Daisy notes early on by stating that "everything's so confused" (147). When Myrtle mistakes Jordan for Tom's wife, Nick tells us that "there is no confusion like the confusion of a simple mind" (157). Myrtle, who earlier saw Tom driving Gatsby's car, mistakes Gatsby and Daisy for Tom and his wife when she sees the yellow car return from the city. Because of this confusion, she leaps into the road to her death.

The confusions and revelations in the chapter lead to two important events. First, they make it possible for

George Wilson (with a nudge from Tom) to mistake Gatsby for Myrtle's lover and to assume it was Gatsby who drove over his wife (when it was actually Daisy), all of which is necessary to enable the tragic ending of the novel. Second, they allow the reader to more accurately judge Daisy's behavior. She is confused and torn between Tom and Gatsby, both of whom are powerful influences over her. Her confusion is heightened by the revelation that Gatsby's money is ill-gotten.

At the close of the chapter, Nick spies Tom and Daisy talking intimately in the pantry. All the confusion leading up to that moment leaves the overwhelming sense that Daisy has surrendered to Tom's will and the inevitability of her social standing. This intensifies our understanding of Gatsby's self-delusion, and fuels the tragedy to come. To lose one's life in the pursuit of true love is noble, but to lose one's life in the pursuit of an illusion is tragic. The seventh chapter shows us Gatsby's self-delusion, which is why Fitzgerald ends it with Gatsby standing in the moonlight outside Tom and Daisy's house, waiting for a signal from Daisy, an act Nick describes as "watching over nothing" (183).

Chapter VIII
In Chapter VIII the tragic fallout from the events of the previous chapter (the *dénouement*) unfolds. Nick visits Gatsby, who had waited all night at Daisy's house to no avail. Gatsby recounts for Nick the romance that caused him to fall in love with Daisy years earlier, and the series of events that took him away from her and how she eventually tired of waiting and married Tom Buchanan. An air of hopelessness floats throughout their conversation, as if the world has awakened from Gatsby's impossible dream of a perfect love.

All the time something within her was cry-
ing for a decision. She wanted her life
shaped now, immediately—and the decision must be made by some force—of
love, of money, of unquestionable practi-
cality—that was close at hand.

That force took shape in the middle of
spring with the arrival of Tom Buchanan.
There was a wholesome bulkiness about
his person and his position, and Daisy was
flattered.

The Great Gatsby (190)

Nick is affected by Gatsby's story, and when Nick
heads off to work, leaving Gatsby, who plans on taking a
swim in the pool, Nick shouts, "They're a rotten crowd.
You're worth the whole damn bunch put together" (193).
At the office, Nick has an uncomfortable conversation
with Jordan and we realize that whatever relationship
they had is over too.

George Wilson's murder/suicide, which is recounted in
this chapter, represents the heart of the novel. Tom sets up
George to believe that Gatsby was Myrtle's lover and that
Gatsby ran her over. This allows Tom to relieve himself of
both George and Gatsby. Tom is off the hook for his affair
with Myrtle and he has eliminated any complications to
his marriage with Daisy. In the previous chapter, Nick
described Tom's predicament as follows: "Tom was feeling the hot whips of panic. His wife and his mistress, until
an hour ago secure and inviolate, were slipping precipi-
tately from his control." (157) Through his manipulation
of George, Tom is able to quickly regain control. He also
avenges Myrtle's death, which he believes was caused by
Gatsby, because he doesn't know that Daisy was driving

the car. It is important to note that Tom suffers no penalty for his actions. He is able to manipulate the lives of those around him without accountability. This is perhaps Fitzgerald's strongest condemnation of the idle upper class.

Chapter IX

The final chapter of *The Great Gatsby* is the novel's most poignant. Here we discover all of the following:

1. The depth of Daisy's self-interest—when we learn that she and Tom have already left East Egg with no plans to return.

2. The extent of Gatsby's commitment to attaining the American Dream—when Gatsby's father shows Nick the worn copy of *Hopalong Cassidy* into the back of which a young Jimmy Gatz (Jay Gatsby) had scribbled a schedule for self-improvement that included practice in elocution and poise.

3. The depth of Tom's indifference to other people—when Nick recalls the next time he ran into Tom, and Tom, without remorse, confirmed Nick's suspicions that he told George Wilson that Gatsby owned the yellow car.

> They were careless people, Tom and Daisy— they smashed up things and creatures and then retreated back into their money or their vast carelessness, or whatever it was that kept them together, and let other people clean up the mess they had made.

> *The Great Gatsby* (226)

4. The scope of Gatsby's solitude—when Nick cannot find anyone to attend Gatsby's funeral, despite the hundreds of people who took advantage of his hospitality.

This fourth point, in particular, helps us to better understand Gatsby's devotion to the ideal he created of Daisy. It may have been that the time Gatsby spent with Daisy was the least lonely period in his life, and for that reason he clung to it despite indications that the time had passed and there was no way to regain it.

The novel ends by referring to Gatsby's desire to return to that privileged moment in his past when Daisy and he first found love, a time symbolized by the green light at the end of Daisy's dock:

> Gatsby believed in the green light, the orgiastic future that year by year recedes before us. It eluded us then, but that's no matter—tomorrow we will run faster, stretch out our arms farther. . . . And one fine morning—
>
> So we beat on, boats against the current, borne back ceaselessly into the past. (228)

In the first chapter of *The Great Gatsby*, it is Gatsby who is gazing toward that green light. In the final chapter, it is Nick. Nick has learned the fallacy of Gatsby's (and his own) desires. In the end, Nick, who has broken off his relationship with Jordan Baker, returns to the simpler Midwest to reacquaint himself with moral certainty. By the end of the novel, we understand what Nick meant at the beginning of the novel when he told us:

> Gatsby turned out all right at the end; it is what preyed on Gatsby, what foul dust floated in the wake of his dreams that temporarily closed out my interest in the abortive sorrows and short-winded elations of men. (5)

The Critical Response to
The Great Gatsby

The initial response to *The Great Gatsby* was good. Many critics recognized that *The Great Gatsby* represented a more mature work than Fitzgerald's previous two novels (*This Side of Paradise* and *The Beautiful and Damned*). Edwin Clark in his *New York Times* review of the novel in 1925 noted that Fitzgerald's "sense of form is becoming perfected." Clark wrote: "Out of this grotesque fusion of incongruities has slowly become conscious a new humor—a strictly American scene. . . . Both boisterous and tragic, it animates this new novel . . . with whimsical magic and simple pathos that is realized with economy and restraint" (Clark 1925, BR9).

A writer for the *New York Post* notes that in writing *The Great Gatsby*, Fitzgerald "definitely deserts his earlier fiction which brought him a lot of money and a certain kind of renown, and enters into the group of American writers who are producing the best serious fiction. On the basis of this book alone Mr. Fitzgerald gives about as much promise as any young writer we have" (Bruccoli, Smith & Kerr 2003, 125).

Laurence Stallings said: "In this new book he [Fitzgerald] is another fellow altogether. 'The great Gatsby' evidences an interest in the color and sweep of prose, in the design and integrity of the novel, in the development of character, like nothing else he has attempted" (Bruccoli, Smith & Kerr 2003, 124).

H. L. Mencken told Fitzgerald that *The Great Gatsby* was "incomparably the best piece of work . . . [he had] done" (Bruccoli, Smith & Kerr 2003, 124). T. S. Eliot, whom Fitzgerald and many others considered the greatest living poet, told Fitzgerald that *Gatsby* was the first major progress in American fiction since the writing of Henry James (Turnbull 1962, 149). Writers Willa Cather and

Edith Wharton praised the work. Conrad Aiken called it a "highly colored and brilliant little novel, which . . . quite escapes the company of most contemporary American fiction" (Aiken 1968, 103).

The Great Gatsby was a critical victory for Fitzgerald, though it failed to sell as well as Fitzgerald had predicted. The novel is arguably Fitzgerald's most artistic work.

Significant Elements of
The Great Gatsby

Fitzgerald identified what he considered to be the primary theme of The Great Gatsby when he told a friend "the whole idea of Gatsby is the unfairness of a poor young man not being able to marry a girl with money. This theme comes up again and again because I lived it" (Turnbull 1962, 150). Late in life he added:

> That was always my experience—a poor boy in a rich town; a poor boy in a rich boy's school; a poor boy in a rich man's club at Princeton. . . . I have never been able to forgive the rich for being rich, and it has colored my entire life and works. (Turnbull 1962, 150)

Like all of Fitzgerald's writing, The Great Gatsby draws heavily on Fitzgerald's life. It is no coincidence that Fitzgerald and Nick Carraway both come from the Midwest, that both Fitzgerald and Gatsby accumulate a great deal of money in a short period of time, that both Fitzgerald and Gatsby loved women who were from a higher socioeconomic class, that both Fitzgerald and Nick Carraway feel as if they are caught between two worlds.

No one-to-one correspondence between Fitzgerald and the people in his life and the characters in The Great

Gatsby can be drawn, but the novel is steeped in autobiographical elements. The character of Nick is much like a young Fitzgerald heading off to New York City to make his fortune as an author. The character of Jay Gatsby shares much with Fitzgerald: Gatsby is in love with a woman from another socioeconomic class just as Fitzgerald was in love with Ginevra King; neither could marry the woman he loved. The parties at Gatsby's mansion are similar to the parties that Fitzgerald threw when he and Zelda lived on Long Island.

Yet *The Great Gatsby* is far more than a well-written confessional. The novel is more than a record of America in the 1920s. It is more than a tragic story of lost love. *The Great Gatsby* resonates with a uniquely American paradox related to the accumulation of wealth and social standing. In America, money provides power, but a move up in economic status involves leaving something behind. Gatsby accumulates wealth, but distances himself from his background and abandons his ethics. He sees Daisy's world as one of possessions and wrongly assumes that in obtaining wealth he will suddenly belong in her world. He sacrifices everything to this end, but it is merely a fantasy. Tom Buchanan and Daisy, who unlike Gatsby were born wealthy, have limited their lives because they are insensitive people. They are trapped by their wealth, and their sensitivity to others suffers. They are careless with other people's lives because they consider themselves superior, not because they are innately evil.

One may view the primary theme of *The Great Gatsby* as the decay or corruption of the American Dream, but it is more accurate to see the novel as debunking the American Dream, since none of the characters in the novel finds any contentment. Characters such as Tom and Daisy Buchanan who are born into money are careless and cruel; those like Gatsby who acquire wealth through their own endeavors are naive and unethical; and those like Nick who fail to achieve their fortune are disillusioned. The most pervasive theme in the novel is how the possession or pursuit of wealth erodes human values.

The Other Novels

THIS SIDE OF PARADISE

F. SCOTT FITZGERALD PUBLISHED *THIS SIDE OF PARADISE*, his first novel, when he was twenty-three, and the work bears the tell-tale marks of a young writer. Yet, it also shows frequent moments of brilliance.

The novel is impressionistic. The events are presented in fragments and scenes chosen for their importance to the main character, Amory Blaine. Amory's point of view dominates the work. Scenes and events are written in various literary styles: narrative, poetry, theatrical drama, and letters.

This Side of Paradise was a commercial success and made Fitzgerald an instant celebrity. Reviews were primarily favorable. What struck readers at the time was the youthful vitality of Fitzgerald's language and the insight the book offered into the new youth of the 1920s. A reviewer for the *New Republic* wrote, "Mr. Fitzgerald has recorded with a good deal of felicity and a disarming frankness the adventures and developments of a curious and fortunate American youth" (Kazin 1951, 48). Burton Rascoe wrote in the *Chicago Tribune*,

> Make a note of the name, F. Scott Fitzgerald. It is borne by a 23 year old novelist who will, unless I am much mistaken, be much heard of hereafter. His first novel, "THIS SIDE OF PARADISE" gives him, I think, a fair claim to membership in that small squad of contemporary American fictionists who are producing literature. (Bruccoli, Smith, & Kerr 2003, 59).

There were bad reviews, too. A reviewer for the *London Times* called the novel "tiresome" (Bruccoli, Smith, and Kerr, p. 59). In his influential biography of Fitzgerald, Arthur Mizener points out that, although young people had been engaging in petting and casual drinking since the teens, "Fitzgerald was the first to describe this life in detail and to represent these activities as new, daring, and admirable" (Mizener 1974, 122). This undoubtedly contributed to the book's appeal in 1920. Readers were enticed by stories of girls who kissed boys to whom they were not engaged. Sy Kahn claims that *This Side of Paradise* is "an allegory in which American Youth is caught between the forces of Good and Evil" (Kahn 1973, 35).

This Side of Paradise recounts the life of Amory Blaine, beginning with his boyhood relationship with his urbane mother, Beatrice, and his experiences at St. Regis prep school, where he neglects his studies. The novel quickly shifts to Amory's collegiate life at Princeton, where he continues his habit of academic idleness, while reading extensively and engaging in pseudophilosophical discussions with his classmates. Before completing his degree, Amory enters military service. His entire experience in World War I is presented in a brief, understated "Interlude," consisting of two letters and a poem.

After the war, Amory falls in love with Rosalind, the sister of his friend Alec Connage. Amory works briefly in New York City at an advertising agency to earn money so that he and Rosalind can be married, but Rosalind breaks off their engagement because Amory is poor. Amory goes on a drinking binge from which he is saved by the start of Prohibition.

Amory has a brief relationship with a woman named Eleanor, who nearly rides her horse over a cliff to prove to Amory that she does not believe in God. Afterward,

Amory loses interest and continues his search for self-awareness on his own. Toward the end of the novel, Rosalind's brother, Alec, is almost caught by hotel detectives with a girl in his room. Amory takes the blame by making it seem that the girl is with him instead. When a small notice of the incident runs in the newspaper, it appears next to a notice of Rosalind's engagement to a wealthy suitor.

Amory takes a walk to Princeton. Along the way he accepts a ride from a wealthy businessman and his associate, with whom he debates philosophical and political ideas. It is after midnight when Amory arrives at Princeton. He muses briefly on his generation, which is "dedicated more than the last to the fear of poverty and the worship of success; grown up to find all Gods dead, all wars fought, all faiths in man shaken" (Fitzgerald 2003, 260). Amory feels as if he has finally come to know himself.

This Side of Paradise is best summarized as Jeffrey Meyers describes it in his biography on Fitzgerald: "It is . . . superficial and immature, but still lively and readable, and valuable both as autobiography and as social history" (Meyers 1994, 56).

The Beautiful and Damned

Edmund Wilson considered Fitzgerald's second novel, *The Beautiful and Damned,* "an advance over *This Side of Paradise,*" claiming that despite the novel's many flaws "the style is more nearly mature and the subject more solidly unified, and there are scenes that are more convincing than any in his other fiction" (in Kazin 1951, 83). Bryant Mangum claims that the novel is "marred by a self-conscious preoccupation with the deterministic philosophy that undergirds American literary naturalism" (Magnum 1988, 514).

The Beautiful and Damned is highly self-conscious

and draws heavily on Fitzgerald and Zelda's relationship. The novel is written in the same impressionistic style as *This Side of Paradise* and also includes sections of drama, poetry, and letters. Its theme, as Sergio Perosa notes, is "the dissipation and deterioration of the inner self" (1965, 36).

The novel is divided into three sections, all dealing with the relationship of Anthony Patch, a wealthy New York heir to an industrial fortune, and Gloria Gilbert, a liberated flapper. In the first section, we are introduced to Anthony, an attractive and intelligent young man of twenty-five, who is the grandson of the wealthy, aging industrialist Adam J. Patch. Anthony is living off the $7,500 a year he derives from interest on his bonds. One of his good friends from Harvard University, Richard "Dick" Caramel, introduces Anthony to his cousin, Gloria Gilbert. Gloria is beautiful and free-spirited and courted by numerous men. Anthony and Gloria go on a few dates while Dick works on his novel, *The Demon Lover*. At the end of the section, Anthony kisses Gloria and declares his love for her.

In Section Two, Anthony and Gloria become engaged. After they are married, they travel and Anthony discovers that Gloria is harder to live with than he had expected. She is particular about the food she will eat, concerned primarily with herself, and not comfortable doing laundry or taking criticism. At one point, Gloria wrecks their car. The accident causes them to chance upon a house for rent in Marietta. They rent the gray house, hire a Japanese servant, and begin throwing parties, drinking, and lounging in the sun. Meanwhile, Dick is becoming a successful writer. Anthony's grandfather is uncomfortable with Anthony's seeming reluctance to work. During a particularly wild party, Anthony's grandfather, an avid moralist, drops in for a visit. He is horrified by the debauchery he witnesses and leaves. Afterward, when Anthony tries to visit him, the elderly man will not see him. A short time later, Anthony's grandfather dies and Anthony, the only close relative, learns that he has been cut out of his grandfather's will—$30 million is left to charity and the remaining $1 million of the estate is left to a man named Shuttleworth, who has been the grandfather's companion. Shuttleworth is also put in charge of dispersing charitable contributions from a large portion of the inheritance. Anthony hires an attorney to contest the will.

The section ends with Gloria being offered work in motion pictures by a man named Bloeckman, who had been a guest in Marietta, and Anthony applying for officer's training after America enters the world war. Gloria refuses the film work and Anthony is rejected for officer's training because he has high blood pressure.

The third section finds Anthony training for the infantry. He is sent to Camp Hooker in South Carolina while Gloria remains in New York City. Anthony starts up an affair with a poorly educated young woman named Dorothy Raycroft, whom he calls "Dot," and Gloria pursues her own interests, reading and volunteer work, often failing to respond to Anthony's letters. When Anthony is transferred to Mississippi, he brings Dot with him and keeps her in a boardinghouse.

After the war, Anthony returns to New York City and he and Gloria rekindle their relationship at an Armistice dance. The cost of an attorney and other expenses have eaten away at their bonds, which are the source of their income, and they find that they now have much less money than before the war. Anthony tries and fails in a half-hearted effort to become a salesman. Bloeckman arranges a screen test for Gloria, but the director says he wants a younger woman. Gloria is devastated at growing older. Anthony gets drunk and embarrasses himself in front of old friends and acquaintances.

TENDER IS THE NIGHT IS ONE OF MANY FITZGERALD NOVELS AND STORIES TO HAVE GOTTEN THE HOLLYWOOD TREATMENT. THIS 1961 HOLLYWOOD PRODUCTION STARRED JASON ROBARDS AND JOAN FONTAINE.

The contesting of the grandfather's will is finally settled. The day Gloria and her cousin Dick, go to find out the final result, Dot shows up at Anthony's door, claiming to love him. He screams at her to leave and throws a chair at her. When Gloria and Dick return with the news that the case has been settled in Anthony's favor and that he is now worth $30 million, they find him studying his childhood stamp collection. His mind has begun to slip.

At the end of the novel, four or five months later, Anthony is alone on the deck of a ship. We learn from casual observers that Shuttleworth committed suicide after losing the case and that Gloria turned against Anthony. In the end, Anthony begins to weep and whispers to himself, "'I showed them. . . . It was a hard fight, but I didn't give up and I came through!'" (Fitzgerald 1998, 370).

The Beautiful and Damned sold well, but Fitzgerald had expected Scribners to sell 60,000 copies in the first year and they only sold 43,000. Still, this was only 1,000 copies less than *This Side of Paradise* had sold during its first year (Turnbull 1962, 132).

Tender Is the Night

Tender Is the Night was Fitzgerald's last complete novel. The manuscript went through numerous drafts over the course of the nine years that passed between publication of *The Great Gatsby* (1925) and its publication in 1934. Reviews of the novel were mixed, although most readers recognized the brilliant sections that mark the book. Ernest Hemingway summed up its quality in a letter to Fitzgerald's editor:

> It's amazing how excellent much of it is. Much of it is better than anything else he ever wrote. How I wish he would have kept on writing. Is it really all over or will

he write again? If you write him give him my great affection. Reading that novel much of it was so good it was frightening. (Bruccoli, Smith, & Kerr 2003, 201).

Malcolm Cowley, writing for the *New Republic*, echoed Hemingway's mixed sense of the work. Cowley writes, "*Tender Is the Night* is a good novel that puzzles you and ends by making you a little angry because it isn't a great novel also. It doesn't give the feeling of being complete in itself. If I didn't like the book so much, I shouldn't have spoken at such length about its shortcomings" (Bruccoli, Smith, & Kerr 2003, 202).

Tender Is the Night deals with the relationship between Dick and Nicole Diver, although it also focuses on other characters on the periphery of their relationship. The novel is divided into three sections. The first section is told from seventeen-year-old American actress Rosemary Hoyt's perspective, and introduces us to Dick and Nicole on the French Riviera during their marriage. The focus of this section is on the first meeting of Dick Diver and Rosemary. Rosemary falls in love with Dick and he—after mild resistance—falls for her, all the while declaring his love for Nicole and insisting that his wife must not be hurt.

Other characters introduced in this section are Tommy Barban, who has an affair with Nicole and marries her after the Divers divorce; Abe North, a musician, and his wife; Albert McKisco, an American novelist, and his wife; Elsie Speers, Rosemary's mother; and two homosexuals: Luis Campion and Royal Dumphry. The section ends when Jules Peterson, an Afro-European who had helped Abe North out of a jam, is found dead in Rosemary's bed. Dick gallantly helps move the body to keep Rosemary out of trouble, and Nicole's mind begins to slip.

The second section jumps back in time and traces Dick Diver's education at Oxford, Johns Hopkins, and another university in Zurich; his service in the war; and the start of his practice as a psychiatrist. We discover that Nicole, who had been molested by her father, was a patient at an asylum in Switzerland when Dick met her. The two exchanged letters, eventually fell in love, and married. They travel a great deal, mostly living on Nicole's money. In 1920, Dick publishes a successful book called *A Psychology for Psychiatrists*.

With money from Nicole's family, Dick goes into partnership with Franz Gregorovius, a pathologist and hypnotist who treated Nicole. The men set up a psychiatric clinic for wealthy patients. After Nicole, in a jealous rage, attempts to crash their car, Dick heads to Munich; then to America for his father's funeral; and finally to Italy, where he once again runs into Rosemary. They argue. Dick goes drinking and winds up in a street brawl that lands him in jail. Nicole's sister bails him out and uses the embarrassing incident as a lever to manipulate him.

Dick's shame follows him back to the clinic where his partner Franz is anxious to buy him out. Eventually, Dick agrees, having "long felt the ethics of his profession dissolving into a lifeless mass" (Fitzgerald 1995, 256). In this, the third and final section of the novel, we watch Dick and Nicole's relationship fall apart. She notes in him a "growing indifference, at present personified by too much drink" (Fitzgerald 1995, 280). Rosemary shows up and we discover that Dick is no longer able to impress her. Tommy and Nicole confront Dick about their love for one another. Nicole says that the marriage had not been the same since Rosemary, and Dick consents to a divorce. He returns to America where he winds up in general practice (rather than psychiatry) and moves to smaller and smaller towns.

THE LAST TYCOON (1976), STARRING ROBERT DENIRO, WAS
NO MORE SUCCESSFUL THAN THE NOVEL.

The Last Tycoon (unfinished)

F. Scott Fitzgerald began work on *The Last Tycoon* in 1939, a year before he died. The eminent critic Edmund Wilson (a friend of Fitzgerald's) shaped a version of Fitzgerald's materials into a novel which was published in 1941, and another version of the materials was edited by Fitzgerald scholar Matthew J. Bruccoli and published in 1993. The novel-in-progress is inspired by the life of movie mogul Irving Thalberg, whom Fitzgerald knew casually from his days in Hollywood.

From the existing drafts of chapters and Fitzgerald's many notes we can surmise that *The Last Tycoon* may have risen to the level of *The Great Gatsby* if Fitzgerald had been able to finish it. A 1941 review of Wilson's edition points to its promise:

> Fitzgerald was a writer, and a born writer, and a writer who strove against considerable odds to widen his range, to improve and sharpen his great technical gifts, and to write a kind of novel that no one else of his generation was able to write. How far he had come along the road to mastery may be seen in this unfinished draft of his last novel. . . . Had Fitzgerald been permitted to finish the book, I think there is no doubt that it would have added a major character and a major novel to American fiction. As it is, "The Last Tycoon" is a great deal more than a fragment. It shows the full powers of its author, at their height and at their best.
>
> (Benét 1941, 10)

Fitzgerald distinguished *The Last Tycoon* from his previous novel in a 1939 letter pitching the idea to

Kenneth Littauer, then editor of *Collier's* magazine. Fitzgerald writes, "Unlike *Tender Is the Night* it is not a story of deterioration—it is not depressing and not morbid in spite of the tragic ending. If one book could ever be 'like' another I should say it is more 'like' *The Great Gatsby* than any other of my books" (Bruccoli 1993, xiii).

Chapter 3

The Short Fiction

ALTHOUGH HE IS MOST COMMONLY thought of as a novelist, Fitzgerald was a prodigious short story writer who published about 160 short stories in his career. These short stories established his fame in the 1920s and provided him with ready income up until the end of his life.

Despite the significance of these short stories to Fitzgerald's body of work, they have been vastly overlooked by critics and scholars. Jackson R. Bryer proposes several overlapping reasons for this oversight (1982). Many of Fitzgerald's short stories were not included in the four short story collections published during Fitzgerald's life, and therefore many are not easily located. In addition, many critics and scholars assumed that most of the short stories were "trash," that they "were simply potboilers written solely and hastily for money" (Bryer 1982, xiii), a claim that Fitzgerald made repeatedly. In a letter to Ernest Hemingway, Fitzgerald compared his writing of short stories with prostitution, referring to himself as an "old whore [at] $4000 a screw" (Bryer 1982, xiii).

John Kuehl points out in his book-length study of Fitzgerald's short fiction that in the early decades of the twentieth century, "mass circulation magazines such as *The Saturday Evening Post* published innumerable stories at high prices, which, since they were 'commercial,' often induced serious craftsmen—Fitzgerald included—to compromise themselves" (Kuel 1991, 3).

Whether one considers Fitzgerald's short stories as great literature in themselves or merely guides to further understand his novels, the better of the stories do show that Fitzgerald knew the craft of the short story and a had masterful command of language.

"Bernice Bobs Her Hair" *(1920)*

"Bernice Bobs Her Hair" was the fourth Fitzgerald story published by *The Saturday Evening Post* (May 1, 1920). It is often included in literary anthologies and provides a clear example of the type of prose that drew mainstream attention and launched Fitzgerald's career.

Fitzgerald's inspiration for the story came from a note he had written to his younger sister, Annabel, in which he offers her advice about how she should behave in order to be popular with boys. The story possesses the quality that writer Raymond Chandler labeled "charm": "He [Fitzgerald] had one of the rarest qualities in all literature . . . charm. . . . It's not a matter of pretty writing or clear style. It's a kind of subdued magic, controlled and exquisite" (Chandler 1986, 239).

"Bernice Bobs Her Hair" focuses on Bernice, an attractive but dull girl visiting Marjorie, her selfish cousin. Bernice, who is not popular with Marjorie's friends, over-hears her cousin complaining about her. Bernice accepts Marjorie's advice on how to be popular, but when she becomes so popular that she threatens to win over Marjorie's best boyfriend, Marjorie tricks her into cutting her hair short ("bobbing"), which hurts her popularity because she is considered "fast," just the effect Marjorie knew it would have. In the end, Bernice heads home early but not before exacting revenge on Marjorie by cutting off her cousin's hair while she sleeps.

A description by Matthew J. Bruccoli of the popularity of Fitzgerald's stories applies well to "Bernice Bobs Her Hair."

> His stories were popular in their time because they were imaginative and surprising—not

because they were predictable. If it can be claimed that the patients who read the *Post* in doctors' waiting rooms responded to brilliant prose and narrative control, then that is what made Fitzgerald a successful magazine writer. He was a natural storyteller; his stories are told in an authorial voice that generates reader confidence. Although the stories are heavily plotted and sometimes utilize trick endings, the main function of the plot is to provide a framework for character. Fitzgerald developed a new American figure: the determined girl-woman. Not the cartoon flapper, but the warm, courageous, attractive, and chastely independent young woman competing at life and love for the highest stakes—her future. Fitzgerald treats his aspiring youths, male and female, seriously and judges them rigorously.

(Bruccoli 1989, xvi)

"Babylon Revisited" *(1931)*

"Babylon Revisited" may be Fitzgerald's best short story, as Carlos Baker noted in his article, "When the Story Ends: 'Babylon Revisited.'" (1982, 269). It is certainly the story that has received the most critical attention. It was first published by *The Saturday Evening Post* on February 21, 1931, and later included in *Taps at Reveille* (1935).

Charlie Wales is returning to Paris years after having lived there with his now deceased wife, Helen, and their daughter Honoria. Charlie was one of the expatriates who earned a great deal of money in the stock market and lived a wild life of waste and excess during the heyday of Paris in the 1920s. At the time of the story, Paris has changed. Many of the free spenders of old lost their fortunes to the stock market crash in 1929. Charlie was an alcoholic whose drinking and revelry got out of hand. One snowy night after a heated argument, he locked his wife Helen out of their apartment. She succumbed to her weak heart and died shortly thereafter. Charlie had gone to a sanitarium and while there had signed over custody of his daughter to his sister-in-law Marion.

By now, Charlie has straightened out his life. He has cut his drinking back to one a day and is employed successfully in Prague. He has come to Paris in the hope of regaining custody of his daughter. He is almost successful, but two acquaintances from his earlier days (using the address that Charlie left with the bartender) show up uninvited at Marion's house. Their drunken behavior appalls Marion and she changes her mind about delivering Honoria over to Charlie. Now he must wait six months instead of a few days before he can possibly reunite with his daughter.

"Babylon Revisited" is an excellent example of the craft of short story writing and of Fitzgerald's consummate skill at the genre. The plot is balanced and tightly organized; the language is concise and poised; and the characters are multidimensional and engaging. Charlie Wales is particularly effective, forging in readers the image of a man who genuinely longs for normality in his life but who is still stigmatized by his earlier folly and heart-wrenching loss.

The story represents a mature look back at Fitzgerald's most common themes about the high living of the 1920s. "In 'Babylon Revisited,'" Sergio Perosa notes, "the tragedy of the Golden Twenties reaches its highest artistic realization" (1965, 96).

"May Day" (1920)

Many refer to "May Day" as Fitzgerald's first great novelette. Matthew J. Bruccoli considers it a masterpiece

(1989, xv). It was first published in *The Smart Set* in July of 1920—Fitzgerald's first year of success as a writer. The story earned Fitzgerald $200, a sizeable sum for the times, but considerably less than *The Saturday Evening Post* would pay him for more light-hearted, popular stories.

"May Day" recounts three overlapping stories, occurring in New York City on May 1st and 2nd. The most central of the three is the story of Gordon Sterrett, a twenty-four-year-old Yale alumnus. Gordon has recently returned from the war and is down on his luck. He has been fired from his job, has no money, and has involved himself with a woman beneath his station (Jewel Hudson), who is blackmailing him for money. In desperation he asks a friend from Yale, Philip Dean, for a loan. Put off by Gordon's pathetic state, Dean refuses to lend him the money he needs, but not before inviting him to a Yale Gamma Psi dance that evening at Delmonico's restaurant. Gordon learns that Edith Bradin, an old flame of his, will be attending the party with Peter Himmel.

The second of the three stories revolves around Edith. She is one of Fitzgerald's flappers. Pretty and carefree, she snubs her escort, Peter, and remembers Gordon as the man she truly loves. But once reunited with him at the dance, she sees Gordon as "pitiful and wretched, a little drunk, and miserably tired" (Fitzgerald, 117), and falls out of love with him, realizing that "love is fragile" (Fitzgerald, 119).

Around 1:30 in the morning, Edith leaves the party to visit her brother, who is working nearby for a socialist newspaper. While visiting him, the office is attacked by an angry mob. During the melee, a soldier, Gus Rose, breaks her brother's leg and Rose's companion, Carrol Key (a fellow soldier), is accidentally shoved out the window and falls to his death. This raid on the fictional *New York Trumpet* mirrors an actual raid on the socialist newspaper

New York Call in 1919 during a heightened period of antisocialism in America.

Rose and Key form the third story. They begin the evening with a search for alcohol. After briefly joining a then small band of riotous men out to seek revenge on socialists, they head for Delmonico's, where Key's brother works as a waiter, to get something to drink. Put off by Edith's rejection of him, Peter heads off to get drunk. He invites Rose and Key to join him as a lark. The two soldiers eventually rejoin the gang and Peter pairs up with Dean for a night of drunken revelry.

Meanwhile, Jewel show up at the dance and insists on seeing Gordon. She claims she cares about him, not the money he was trying to borrow for her, and drags him away from the dance.

In the morning, Gordon awakes to discover that he is "irrevocably married to Jewel Hudson" (Fitzgerald 1989, 141). He buys a revolver, goes back to his apartment, and shoots himself in the head.

"May Day" demonstrates Fitzgerald's skill at creating atmosphere. His prose contrasts the exhilaration of postwar America with the disillusionment that many men felt after returning home to discover a great divide between those with and those without wealth. Fitzgerald beautifully balances the drunken merriment of Mr. In and Mr. Out (Peter and Dean) with the harshness of Gordon's suicide.

"Winter Dreams" *(1922)*

Fitzgerald called "Winter Dreams" "a sort of first draft of the Gatsby idea" (Turnbull 1962, 133). Matthew Bruccoli calls it "the strongest" of the Fitzgerald stories that foreshadow *The Great Gatsby*. It was published in *Metropolitan Magazine* in 1922 and later collected in *All the Sad Young Men* (1926).

"Winter Dreams" recounts Dexter Green's infatuation with a young debutante named Judy Jones, beginning in

Minnesota when Dexter is fourteen and ending in New York City when he is thirty-two. Like Daisy Fay in *The Great Gatsby*, Judy, a beautiful flirt, draws men to her, toying with their affections. Dexter becomes captivated by her beauty and joins the ranks of her many suitors. Although he is already a successful businessman, he cannot capture Judy for himself. He abandons his pursuit of her after a year and a half and eventually becomes engaged to a more suitable woman (Irene Scheerer), only to throw her over the moment Judy reappears in his life and proposes marriage. The romantic reunion only lasts one month, but Dexter has no regrets about his decision to break it off with Irene for a brief time with Judy.

The story ends seven years later when Dexter learns from a business acquaintance (Devlin) that Judy's beauty has faded, ending his illusions of "youth" and the "richness of life" (Fitzgerald 1989, 236). Dexter explains his disillusionment to Devlin:

> "Long ago," he said, "long ago, there was something in me, but now that thing is gone. Now that this is gone, that thing is gone. I cannot cry. I cannot care. That thing will come back no more." (Fitzgerald 1989, 236)

Chapter 4

Other Writings

F. SCOTT FITZGERALD'S REPUTATION as a great American author rests on his work first as a novelist and then as a short story writer, but these were not the only genres in which he wrote. As a boy and young man, he wrote plays and poetry. Sergio Perosa notes that Fitzgerald's work as a juvenile "consist[s] of sixteen short stories, nine poems, five book reviews, a dozen satirical and humorous pieces, four little plays, and the ideas and lyrics for three musical shows" (Perosa 1965, 12).

He was also enamored of musical theater, and at Princeton contributed a number of lyrics to musical productions. Later in life, he wrote Hollywood screenplays.

Articles and Essays

Fitzgerald wrote essays throughout his career, beginning with articles for St. Paul Academy's *Now and Then* and the *Newman News* when he was a young man to later articles for *The Saturday Evening Post*, *The Princeton Alumni Weekly*, *The New Yorker*, *The Ladies' Home Journal*, *Scribner's Magazine*, *Esquire*, and a variety of other periodicals. Many have enticing titles such as "'Why Blame It on the Poor Kiss if the Girl Veteran of Many Petting Parties Is Prone to Affairs After Marriage?'" (*New York American*, February 24, 1924) and "How to Live on $36,000 a Year" (*The Saturday Evening Post*, April 5, 1924), and most provide insight into the life and mind of the author. The most significant of these essays to an understanding of Fitzgerald's later life is arguably "The

Crack-Up." Fitzgerald wrote the essay when he was living in "the wave of despair which followed" (Turnbull 1962, 270) the Jazz Age.

"The Crack-Up" (1936)

Many stories from Fitzgerald's final years, such as "The Lost Decade" and the Pat Hobby stories (written in the last year of Fitzgerald's life), convey a powerful sense of loss. "The Lost Decade," for example, recounts the story of Louis Trimble, a once-successful architect who spent the last ten years drunk. Now sober, he revisits New York, a city he helped to design.

"The Crack-Up" provides an excellent view of Fitzgerald's mind when his fame and success were in decline and he was battling powerful feelings of disappointment, alienation, and failure.

The essay was first published in *Esquire* in February of 1936. It begins:

> Of course all life is a process of breaking down, but the blows that do the dramatic side of the work—the big sudden blows that come or seem to come, from outside— the ones you remember and blame things on and, in moments of weakness, tell your friends about, don't show their effect all at once. There is another sort of blow that comes from within—that you don't feel until it's too late to do anything about it, until you realize with finality that in some regard you will never be as good a man again. The first sort of breakage seems to happen quick—the second kind happens almost without your knowing it but is realized suddenly indeed. (Fitzgerald, 405)

"The Crack-Up" paints a tragic image for readers. Fitzgerald might have recovered his literary grace if he had not died at such a young age, but as his life played out, he was a man removed from his most vibrant and successful decade. Fitzgerald passed from his twenties into his thirties and "The Jazz Age" followed him. They both came in the 1930s to be regarded with nostalgia as fads—like the Charleston, dance marathons, and flappers—that had passed and were no longer relevant.

Poetry and Song Lyrics

Fitzgerald wrote poetry and lyrics only occasionally; nevertheless he felt very strongly about poetry, as he makes clear in the following sentence from a letter he wrote to his daughter, Scottie: "Poetry is either something that lives like fire inside you—like music to the musician or Marxism to the communist—or else it is nothing, an empty, formalized bore." (Fitzgerald 1981, xi).

Despite his awareness of the importance of poetry and his appreciation for the work of great poets, Fitzgerald's poetry seldom achieves brilliance. It does play a role in his fiction, with poems scattered throughout *This Side of Paradise*, *The Beautiful and Damned*, and other works.

Fitzgerald published about twenty-four poems during his career, such as the following example from *The New Yorker* magazine (March 23, 1935) about his life with Zelda before his illness:

Lamp in a Window

Do you remember, before keys turned in the locks,
When life was a closeup, and not an occasional letter,
That I hated to swim naked from the rocks
While you liked absolutely nothing better?

Do you remember many hotel bureaus that had
Only three drawers? But the only trouble

Was that each of us got holy, then got mad
Trying to give the third one to the other.

East, west, the little car turned, often wrong
Up an erroneous Alp, an unmapped Savoy river.
We blamed each other, wild were our words and strong,
And, in an hour, laughed and called it liver.

And, though the end was desolate and unkind:
To turn the calendar at June and find December
On the next leaf; still, stupid-got with grief, I find
These are the only quarrels that I can remember.

Most of Fitzgerald's song lyrics date back to his days at Princeton or are brief snippets from his notebooks. As a lyricist, Fitzgerald fares better than he does as a poet; however, nearly all his work is from his days as a youth and a student at Princeton. Still, song lyrics tend to place more importance on wit and cleverness than poetry, and in Fitzgerald's song lyrics there are glimpses of wit. In "Is It Art?" from the musical *Safety First*, Fitzgerald pokes fun at modern art, as evident in the following passage from the first verse:

There are no strict requirements for a cubist,
You only need a dipper full of paint,
A little distance bring it
And at your canvas fling it,
Then shut your eyes and name it what it ain't.

Stage Plays and Screenplays

Most of Fitzgerald's plays date from his youth. He "had always loved plays," and, inspired by a school production of "A Regular Fix" (Mizener 1973, 47), Fitzgerald wrote his first play, "The Girl From Lazy J," in 1911 at the age of fourteen. He wrote three more produced plays before leaving for Princeton in 1914. At Princeton he published plays in the *Nassau Literary Magazine* (while writing lyrics for Triangle Club productions).

Once Fitzgerald began to earn a living as a writer, his interest in theater took a back seat to his more profitable novels and short stories. Nevertheless, his interest is still evident. Both of his first two novels, *This Side of Paradise* and *The Beautiful and Damned*, have sections that are formatted like plays. In 1923 he wrote *The Vegetable*, which was produced but bombed.

Fitzgerald's interest in screenwriting emerged at the beginning of his writing career. No sooner had Fitzgerald acquired literary agent Harold Ober than he was asking him if money could be made writing for the movies. He wrote three scenarios (as screenplays were referred to in the early days of cinema) around the time he published his first novel, *This Side of Paradise*, and he toured the Mamaroneck, New York, studios of D. W. Griffith in 1920. In 1922 Fitzgerald wrote an outline for *Transcontinental Kitty* at the request of David O. Selznick. Selznick disliked the treatment and the project was abandoned. As Gene D. Phillips notes, "Fitzgerald never became particularly proficient at writing screenplays" (1986, 13).

After achieving fame, Fitzgerald was courted by Hollywood despite his earlier failures as a screenwriter. He did not have good experiences there and he looked upon screenwriting primarily as a way to make money. Toward the end of his life, he turned to Hollywood in desperation to try and earn a living. He worked as a contract writer for MGM for a year and a half during 1937 and 1938. When MGM did not renew his contract, he freelanced until his death in 1940. Fitzgerald worked on a number of screenplays, including *Gone with the Wind*, *Lipstick*, and *A Yank at Oxford*, but he received a screen credit for only one film—*Three Comrades*. Part of the problem may have been Fitzgerald's difficulty adapting to the form. As film director Billy Wilder put it, "He made me think of a great sculptor who is hired to do a plumbing job. He did not know how to connect the pipes so that the water would flow" (Zolotow 1977, 72).

Although Fitzgerald never mastered the genre of the screenplay, he did take "screenwriting very seriously," as Matthew J. Bruccoli noted when commenting on 2,000 pages of Fitzgerald manuscripts (most from his days as a screenwriter) which were purchased by the Thomas Cooper Library of the University of South Carolina. Bruccoli adds, "it's heartbreaking to see how much effort he put into it" (McGrath, 2004).

Chronology

1896
F. Scott Fitzgerald is born in St. Paul, Minnesota, on September 24.

1908
Enters St. Paul Academy in St. Paul, Minnesota.

1909
Publishes for the first time. "The Mystery of the Raymond Mortgage" appears in *Now and Then*, a publication of St. Paul Academy.

1911
First play produced at St. Paul. It is called *The Girl from Lazy J*.
Enters the Newman School in Hackensack, New Jersey.

1912
Second play produced: *The Captured Shadow.*

1913
Third play, *Coward*, produced in St. Paul.
Enters Princeton University.

1914
Fourth play, *Assorted Spirits*, produced in St. Paul.
Begins writing for the *Princeton Tiger*.

The Triangle Club at Princeton puts on a production of *Fie! Fie! Fi-Fi!*, for which Fitzgerald contributed song lyrics and assisted in the production.

1915
Nassau Literary Magazine publishes Fitzgerald's play, *Shadow Laurels.*
Nassau Literary Magazine publishes Fitzgerald's short story, "The Ordeal."
Struggling with his grades, Fitzgerald drops out of Princeton in November.
In December, the Triangle Club performs *The Evil Eye*, with song lyrics by Fitzgerald.

1916
Returns to Princeton in September, and is told he must repeat his junior year.
In December, the Triangle Club performs *Safety First*, with song lyrics by Fitzgerald.

1917
Receives a commission as a second lieutenant in the infantry.
Arrives at Fort Leavenworth, Kansas in, November.
Begins work on a novel titled *The Romantic Egotist.*

1918
Meets Zelda Sayre.
Scribners returns Fitzgerald's novel, *The Romantic Egotist*, in August with suggestions for revision. Fitzgerald revises the manuscript. This time Scribners reject the manuscript outright.

1919
In September, Fitzgerald garners his first commercial publication when *The Smart Set* publishes "Babes in the

Woods." That same month, Scribners accepts his novel, now titled *This Side of Paradise*, for publication.
In October, sells his first story ("Head and Shoulders") to the *Saturday Evening Post*, establishing a profitable connection to the magazine that would long serve him as a source of income and be instrumental in building his reputation.

1920
This Side of Paradise is published in March.
On April 3, Fitzgerald and Zelda Sayre are married at St. Patrick's Cathedral in New York.
In September, a collection of his short stories is published under the title *Flappers and Philosophers*.

1921
On October 26, their daughter Frances Scott "Scottie" Fitzgerald is born.

1922
The Beautiful and Damned is published.
In September, a second collection of his short stories is published under the title *Tales of the Jazz Age*.

1923
Publishes a play, *The Vegetable*.

1925
The Great Gatsby is published.

1926
Owen Davis adapts *The Great Gatsby* for the stage. The play opens on Broadway in February.
Third collection of short stories is published under the title *All the Sad Young Men*.

1928
Fitzgeralds sail to Paris.
The Saturday Evening Post begins the publication of eight stories from Fitzgerald's Basil Duke Lee series.

1932
Zelda's novel, *Save Me the Waltz*, is published in October.
Zelda is admitted to Phipps Psychiatric Clinic of Johns Hopkins University Hospital, Baltimore, suffering from hallucinations.

1934
Scribners Magazine begins the serialized publication of *Tender Is the Night*.
In April, *Tender Is the Night* is published.
Zelda is transferred to Sheppard-Pratt Hospital, and then to Craig House Hospital.

1935
Another collection of Fitzgerald's short stories is published under the title *Taps at Reveille*.

1936
Zelda transferred to Highland Hospital, Asheville, North Carolina.

1937
Returns to Hollywood with a six-month contract to write for MGM.
One week after arriving, meets Sheilah Graham. The two begin a relationship that will last the rest of Fitzgerald's life.
In December, Fitzgerald's contract is renewed for another year.

1939
In the summer, begins work on *The Last Tycoon*, based loosely on the life of movie mogul Irving Thalberg.

1940
Begins publishing his Pat Hobby stories in *Esquire*. Suffers a fatal heart attack in Sheilah Graham's apartment on December 21. Buried in Rockville Union Cemetery, Rockville, Maryland, on December 27.

1941
His unfinished novel, *The Last Tycoon*, is published.

1948
Zelda dies in a fire at Highland Hospital on March 10. Zelda is buried next to Scott on March 17.

1975
On November 7, Scott and Zelda are moved to St. Mary's Catholic Church Cemetery, Rockville, Maryland, and reburied in the Fitzgerald family plot.

Novels

THIS SIDE OF PARADISE. NEW YORK: SCRIBNERS, 1920.

THE BEAUTFIUL AND DAMNED. NEW YORK: SCRIBNERS, 1922; LONDON: COLLINS, 1922.

THE GREAT GATSBY. NEW YORK: SCRIBNERS, 1925; LONDON: CHATTO AND WINDUS, 1926.

TENDER IS THE NIGHT. NEW YORK: SCRIBNERS, 1934; LONDON: CHATTO AND WINDUS, 1934.

THE LAST TYCOON. NEW YORK: SCRIBNERS, 1941; LONDON: GREY WALLS, 1949.

Short Story Collections

Flappers and Philosophers. New York: Scribners, 1920; London: Collins, 1922.

Tales of the Jazz Age. New York: Scribners, 1922; London: Collins, 1923.

All the Sad Young Men. New York: Scribners, 1926.

Taps at Reveille. New York: Scribners, 1935.

The Stories of F. Scott Fitzgerald. Ed. Malcolm Cowley. New York: Scribners, 1951.

Afternoon of an Author. Ed. Arthur Mizener. Princeton, NJ: Princeton University Library, 1957.

The Pat Hobby Stories. Ed. Arnold Gingrich. New York: Scribners, 1962.

The Apprentice Fiction of F. Scott Fitzgerald. Ed. John Kuehl. New Brunswick, NJ: Rutgers University Press, 1965.

The Basil and Josephine Stories. Ed. Jackson R. Bryer and John Kuehl. New York: Scribners, 1973.

Bits of Paradise. Ed. Matthew J. Bruccoli and Scottie Fitzgerald Smith. London: Bodley Head, 1973; New York: Scribners, 1973.

The Price Was High. Ed. Matthew J. Bruccoli. New York and London: Harcourt Brace Jovanovich/Bruccoli Clark, 1979.

The Short Stories of F. Scott Fitzgerald. Ed. Matthew J. Bruccoli. New York: Scribners, 1989.

Before Gatsby: The First Twenty-Six Stories. Ed. Matthew J. Bruccoli & Judith S. Baughman. Columbia: University of South Carolina Press, 2001.

Papers and Notebooks
The Crack-Up. Ed. Edmund Wilson. New York: New Directions, 1945.

Plays
The Vegetable. New York: Scribners, 1923.
F. Scott Fitzgerald's St. Paul Plays. Ed. Alan Margolies. Princeton, NJ: Princeton University Library, 1978.

Screenplays

F. Scott Fitzgerald's Screenplay for Erich Maria Remarque's Three Comrades. Ed. Matthew J. Bruccoli. Carbondale and Edwardsville: Southern Illinois University Press, 1978.

Babylon Revisited: The Screenplay. New York: Carroll and Graf, 1993.

Poetry

Poems 1911–1940. Ed. Matthew J. Bruccoli. Bloomfield Hills, MI, and Columbia, SC: Bruccoli, Clark, 1981.

Song Lyrics

Fie! Fie! Fi-Fi! Cincinnati, New York and London: The John Church Co., 1914. (A collection of lyrics to seventeen songs).

The Evil Eye. Cincinnati, New York and London: The John Church Co., 1915. (A collection of lyrics to seventeen songs).

Safety First. Cincinnati, New York and London: The John Church Co., 1916. (A collection of lyrics to seventeen songs).

Essays

The Cruise of the Rolling Junk. Bloomfield Hills, MI, and Columbia SC: Bruccoli, Clark, 1976.

F. Scott Fitzgerald on Authorship. Ed. Matthew J. Bruccoli, with Judith S. Baughman. Columbia: University of South Carolina Press, 1996.

Letters & Miscellaneous Publications

The Letters of F. Scott Fitzgerald. Ed. Andrew Turnbull. New York: Scribners, 1964.

Thoughtbook of Francis Scott Key Fitzgerald. Ed. John Kuehl. Princeton, NJ: Princeton University Library, 1965.

F. Scott Fitzgerald: The Princeton Years: Selected Writings, 1914–1920. Ed. Chip Deffaa. Fort Bragg, CA: Cypress House Press, 1966.

F. Scott Fitzgerald in His Own Time: A Miscellany. Ed. Matthew J. Bruccoli, and Jackson R. Bryer. Kent, OH: Kent State University Press, 1971.

Dear Scott/Dear Max: The Fitzgerald–Perkins Correspondence. Ed. John Kuehl and Jackson R. Bryer. New York: Scribners, 1971.

As Ever, Scott Fitz——: Letters between F. Scott Fitzgerald and His Literary Agent Harold Ober 1919–1940. Ed. Matthew J. Bruccoli, and Jennifer M. Atkinson. Philadelphia and New York: J. B. Lippincott, 1972.

F. Scott Fitzgerald's Ledger (A Facsimile). Ed. Matthew J. Bruccoli. Washington: Bruccoli Clark/NCR, 1973.

The Notebooks of F. Scott Fitzgerald. Ed. Matthew J. Bruccoli, New York and London: Harcourt Brace Jovanovich/Bruccoli Clark, 1978.

Correspondence of F. Scott Fitzgerald. Ed. Matthew J. Bruccoli and Margaret M. Duggan, with Susan Walker. New York: Random House, 1980.

F. Scott Fitzgerald: Inscriptions. Columbia, SC: Matthew J. Bruccoli, 1988.

F. Scott Fitzgerald: A Life in Letters. Ed. Matthew J. Bruccoli, with Judith S. Baughman. New York: Scribners, 1994.

Trimalchio: A Facsimile Edition of the Original Galley Proofs for The Great Gatsby. Columbia: University of South Carolina Press, 2000.

Dear Scott, Dearest Zelda: The Love Letters of F. Scott Fitzgerald and Zelda Fitzgerald. Eds. Jackson R Bryer, and Cathy W. Barks. New York: St. Martin's Press, 2002.

The Chorus Girl's Romance. Dir. William C. Dowlan. Based on story by F. Scott Fitzgerald ("Head and Shoulders"). Screenplay by Percy Heath. 1920.

The Husband Hunter. Dir. Howard M. Mitchell. Based on story by F. Scott Fitzgerald ("Myra Meets His Family"). Scenario by Joseph F. Poland. 1920.

The Off-Shore Pirate. Dir. Dallas M. Fitzgerald. Story by F. Scott Fitzgerald. Adapted by Waldemar Young. 1921.

The Beautiful and Damned. Dir. William A. Seiter. Based on the novel by F. Scott Fitzgerald. Screenplay by Olga Printzlau. 1922.

The Glimpses of the Moon (uncredited). Dir. Allan Dwan. Based on a novel by Edith Wharton. 1923.

Grit. Dir. Frank Tuttle. Based on a story by F. Scott Fitzgerald. Screenplay by James Ashmore Creelman. 1924.

The Great Gatsby. Dir. Herbert Brenon. Based on the novel by F. Scott Fitzgerald. Screenplay by Becky Gardiner and Elizabeth Meehan. 1926.

Pusher-in-the-Face (uncredited). Dir. Robert Florey. 1929.

Raffles (uncredited). Dir. George Fitzmaurice. Based on a play by Eugene Wiley Presbrey. 1930.

Red-Headed Woman (uncredited). Dir. Jack Conway. Based on a novel by Katherine Brush. 1932.

A Yank in Oxford (uncredited, worked on treatment). Dir. Jack Conway. Based on an idea by John Monk Saunders. 1938.

Three Comrades. Dir. Frank Borzage. Based on a novel by Erich Maria Remarque. Screenplay by F. Scott Fitzgerald and Edward E. Paramore, Jr. 1938.

Marie Antoinette (uncredited). Dir. W.S. Van Dyke. 1938.

Winter Carnival (uncredited). Dir. Charles Reisner. 1939.

The Women (uncredited). Dir. George Cukor. Based on a play by Clare Booth Luce. 1939.

Honeymoon in Bali (uncredited). Dir. Edward H. Griffith. 1939.

Gone with the Wind (uncredited). Dir. Victor Fleming. Based on a novel by Margaret Mitchell. 1939.

Everything Happens at Night (uncredited). Dir. Irving Cummings. 1939.

Raffles (remake of 1930 screenplay, uncredited). Dir. Sam Wood. Based on a play by Eugene Wiley Presbrey. 1940.

Life Begins at Eight-Thirty (uncredited). Dir. Irving Pichel. Based on a play by Emlyn Williams. 1942.

The Great Gatsby. Dir. Elliot Nugent. Based on the novel by F. Scott Fitzgerald and the play adaptation by Owen Davis. 1949.

The Last Time I Saw Paris. Dir. Richard Brooks. Story by F. Scott Fitzgerald. Screenplay by Julius J. Epstein, Philip G. Epstein, and Richard Brooks. 1954.

Tender Is the Night. Dir. Henry King. Based on the novel by F. Scott Fitzgerald. Screenplay by Ivan Moffat. 1962.

The Great Gatsby. Dir. Jack Clayton. Based on the novel by F. Scott Fitzgerald. Screenplay by Francis Ford Coppola. 1974.

The Last Tycoon. Dir. Elia Kazan. Based on the novel by F. Scott Fitzgerald. Screenplay by Harold Pinter. 1976.

Tender Is the Night (television miniseries). Dir. Robert Knights. Based on Malcolm Cowley's 1951 re-editing of the novel by F. Scott Fitzgerald. Screenplay by Dennis Potter. 1985.

The Great Gatsby (television movie). Dir. Robert Markowitz. Based on the novel by F. Scott Fitzgerald. Teleplay by John McLaughlin. 2000.

* Productions marked "uncredited" indicate Fitzgerald worked on the screenplay or story, but did not receive a screen credit.

p. 22, Fitzgerald had met Shane Leslie when Leslie visited the Newman School where he was a student.

p. 23, See Nancy Milford's biography of Zelda Fitzgerald's life (Milford 1970, 35, et passim).

p. 26, Lyric from "Anything Goes" by Cole Porter.

pp. 27–28, From a letter to Maxwell Perkins written just prior to May 21, 1931. (Turnbull 1963, 225).

p. 31, Gerald Murphy was one of Fitzgerald's models for Dick Diver, a principal character in *Tender Is the Night*.

p. 32, At the time of their meeting, a story by Ernest Hemingway sold for around forty dollars while a story by F. Scott Fitzgerald sold for several thousand dollars.

p. 34, There is some irony in Scott's condemnation of Zelda's dependence on him since some of Zelda's writing had already begun to appear in print under his name.

p. 35, For example, the story "The Changing Beauty of Park Avenue" was written solely by Zelda, a point Scott notes in his ledger; yet, Scott added both their names to the title, placing his name first. (Milford 1970, 132). Scott added his name to Zelda's works to insure that they would sell and to increase the amount of money they earned.

p. 38, The house was located at 919 Felder Avenue, the current site of the F. Scott Fitzgerald and Zelda Fitzgerald Museum.

p. 40, F. Scott Fitzgerald's name was removed from later versions of the story; the character's name was changed to Julian.

p. 48, By comparison, in 1928 the United Kingdom manufactured only 212,000 automobiles, France made 210,000, and Canada 242,000.

p. 54, Seneca Falls, New York, was the location of the first public women's rights convention held in the United States. The meeting was organized by Elizabeth Cady Stanton and Lucretia Mott. It marked the official beginning of the American feminist movement.

p. 55, Consider Ernest Hemingway, who spent twenty years living in Cuba and who, toward the end of his life, kissed the edge of the Cuban flag and claimed to be Cuban.

p. 57, Even here there is difficulty in that Fitzgerald very much agreed with established notions of class.

p. 60, According to Jackson R. Bryer, Fitzgerald published 146 short stories in his career, but he wrote 178 stories. (Bryer 1982, xi).

p. 70, A term used for the newly rich. It distinguishes them from people who descend from families that have been wealthy for generations.

p. 82, Critic Milton R. Stern points out parallels between Nick and Jordan's relationship and Gatsby and Daisy's relationship and claims that Nick breaks with Jordan because she "abandons Tom and Daisy, after having lived with and off them, in order to not be involved in their troubles." This, Stern argues, is a "very Tom-and-Daisyish thing to do." (Stern 1970, 209).

Further Reading

Bloom, Harold. *F. Scott Fitzgerald*. New York: Chelsea House Publications, 1999.

Jazz Age: The 20s, The. New York: Time-Life Books, 1998.

Mizener, Arthur. *The Far Side of Paradise* (Biography). New York: Avon, 1974.

Tate, Mary Jo. *F. Scott Fitzgerald A to Z*. New York: Facts on File, 1999.

Turnbull, Andrew. *Scott Fitzgerald* (Biography). New York: Scribners, 1962.

Weisbrod, Eva. *A Student's Guide to F. Scott Fitzgerald*. Berkeley Heights, NJ: Enslow Publishers, 2004.

Web Sites

F. Scott Fitzgerald Centenary Web site, University of South Carolina
http://www.sc.edu/fitzgerald/

The F. Scott Fitzgerald Society Website
http://www.fitzgeraldsociety.org/

F. Scott Fitzgerald and Zelda Fitzgerald Background
http://www.zeldafitzgerald.com/fitzgeralds/index.asp

New York Times Featured Author page on F. Scott Fitzgerald
http://partners.nytimes.com/books/00/12/24/specials/
fitzgerald.html

PBS biographies on F. Scott and Zelda Fitzgerald
http://www.pbs.org/kteh/amstorytellers/bios.html

Aiken, Conrad. "F. Scott Fitzgerald." *Twentieth Century Interpretations of The Great Gatsby*. Ed. Ernest Lockridge. Englewood Cliffs, NJ: Prentice Hall, 1968.

Baker, Carlos. "When the Story Ends: 'Babylon Revisited.'" *The Short Stories of F. Scott Fitzgerald: New Approaches in Criticism*. Ed. Jackson R. Bryer. Madison, WI: University of Wisconsin Press, 1982.

Benét, Stephen Vincent. Review of *The Last Tycoon*. *The Saturday Review of Literature* 24 (6 December 1941): 10.

Broun, Heywood. *The New York Tribune* (May 7, 1920). Reprinted in *Conversations with F. Scott Fitzgerald*.

Bruccoli, Matthew J. "Preface." *The Last Tycoon*. New York: Scribner, 1993.

_____. "Preface." *The Great Gatsby: The Authorized Text*. New York: Simon & Schuster, 1995.

_____. "Preface." *The Short Stories of F. Scott Fitzgerald*. New York: Scribner, 1989.

Bruccoli, Matthew J., Scottie Fitzgerald Smith, and Joan P. Kerr, eds. *The Romantic Egoists: A Pictorial Autobiography from the Scrapbooks and Albums of F. Scott and Zelda Fitzgerald*. Columbia, University of South Carolina Press, 2003.

Bruccoli, Matthew J., and Judith S. Baughman, eds. *Conversations with F. Scott Fitzgerald*. Jackson: University Press of Mississippi, 2004.

Bryer, Jackson R., ed. *The Short Stories of F. Scott Fitzgerald: New Approaches in Criticism*. Madison, Wisconsin: University of Wisconsin Press, 1982.

Bryer, Jackson R., and Cathy W. Barks, eds. *Dear Scott, Dearest Zelda: The Love Letters of F. Scott Fitzgerald and Zelda Fitzgerald*. New York: St. Martin's Press, 2002.

Chambers, John B. *The Novels of F. Scott Fitzgerald*. New York: St. Martin's Press, 1989.

Clark, Edwin. "Scott Fitzgerald Looks Into Middle Age." *New York Times,* April 19, 1925: BR9.

Dolan, Marc. *Modern Lives: A Cultural Re-reading of "The Lost Generation."* West Lafayette, IN: Purdue University Press, 1996.

Fitzgerald, F. Scott. *The Beautiful and Damned*. New York: Penguin, 1998.

_____. *The Great Gatsby*. Upper Saddle River, NJ: Prentice Hall, 1968.

_____. *The Last Tycoon*. New York: Scribner, 1941.

_____. *The Last Tycoon: The Authorized Text*. Ed. Matthew J. Bruccoli. New York: Scribner, 1993.

_____. *Poems: 1911–1940*. Ed. Matthew J. Bruccoli. Bloomfield Hills, MI & Columbia, SC: Bruccoli Clark, 1981.

_____. *The Short Stories of F. Scott Fitzgerald*. Ed. Matthew J. Bruccoli. New York: Scribner, 1989.

_____. *This Side of Paradise*. New York: Scribner, 2003.

_____. *Tender Is the Night*. New York: Simon & Schuster, 1995.

Flanagan, Thomas. "Fitzgerald's 'Radiant World.'" *The New York Review of Books*, v. 47 n. 20. December 21, 2000. http://www.nybooks.com/articles/13917 (Accessed July 10, 2004).

Hook, Andrew. *F. Scott Fitzgerald*. London: Edward Arnold, 1992.

Kahn, Sy. "*This Side of Paradise*: The Pageantry of Disillusion." *F. Scott Fitzgerald: A Collection of Criticism*. Ed. Kenneth E. Eble. New York: McGraw-Hill, 1973.

Kallen, Stuart A., ed. *The Roaring Twenties*. San Diego, CA: Greenhaven Press, 2002.

Kazin, Alfred, ed. *F. Scott Fitzgerald: The Man and His Work*. New York: World Publishing Company, 1951.

Kuehl, John. *F. Scott Fitzgerald: A Study of the Short Fiction*. Boston: Twayne, 1991.

Lockridge, Ernest, ed. *Twentieth Century Interpretations of The Great Gatsby*. Englewood Cliffs, NJ: Prentice Hall, 1968.

Mangum, Bryant. *The Great Gatsby, Encyclopedia of the Novel*. Ed. Paul Schellinger. Chicago and London: Fitzroy-Dearborn, 1988.

McGrath, Charles. "No Hollywood Ending for Fitzgerald, Papers Show." *The New York Times, April 22, 2004.*

Meyers, Jeffrey. *Scott Fitzgerald.* New York: Harper Collins, 1994.

Milford, Nancy. *Zelda: A Biography.* New York: Harper & Row, 1970.

Mizener, Arthur. "Scott Fitzgerald and the 1920's." *F. Scott Fitzgerald: A Collection of Criticism.* Ed. Kenneth E. Eble. New York: McGraw Hill, 1973.

_____. *The Far Side of Paradise.* New York: Avon, 1974. Oxford English Dictionary. OED Online. 24 October 2004. http://dictionary.oed.com

Panati, Charles. *Panati's Parade of Fads, Follies, and Manias: The Origins of Our Most Cherished Obsessions.* New York: Harper Perennial, 1991.

Perosa, Sergio. *The Art of F. Scott Fitzgerald.* Trans. Charles Matz and Sergio Perosa. Ann Arbor: University of Michigan Press, 1965.

Phillips, Gene D. *Fiction, Film, and F. Scott Fitzgerald.* Chicago: Loyola University Press, 1986.

Stern, Milton R. *The Golden Moment: The Novels of F. Scott Fitzgerald.* Urbana, IL: University of Illinois Press, 1970.

Stevens, Ruth. "Before Zelda, there was Ginevra." *Princeton Alumni Weekly Bulletin* 93.1 7 Sept. 2003. 29 June 2004. http://www.princeton.edu/pr/pwb/03/0907/1c.shtml

Streissguth, Tom. *The Roaring Twenties: An Eyewitness History.* New York: Facts on File, 2001.

Turnbull, Andrew. *Scott Fitzgerald (Biography).* New York: Scribner, 1962.

_____. ed. *The Letters of F. Scott Fitzgerald.* New York: Scribner, 1963.

Zolotow, Maurice. *Billy Wilder in Hollywood.* New York: Putnam, 1977.

Index

Page numbers in **boldface** are illustrations. A (c) denotes fictional character. An (f) denotes fictional location.

About the Author

Kevin A. Boon is an assistant professor at Penn State University and English Program Coordinator for the Mount Alto campus. He teaches film, writing, and literature, and is the author and editor of a number of books on Kurt Vonnegut, Virginia Woolf, and other writers. He is also an award-winning poet and fiction writer, a skilled composer and musician, and a playwright.